Nazi Germany 1930–1939

GCSE Modern World History for Edexcel

Steve Waugh

John Wright

A MEMBER OF THE HODDER HEADLINE GROUP

This high quality material is endorsed by Edexcel and has been through a rigorous quality assurance programme to ensure that it is a suitable companion to the specification for both learners and teachers. This does not mean that its contents will be used verbatim when setting examinations nor is it to be read as being the official specification – a copy of which is available at www.edexcel.org.uk.

The Publishers would like to thank the following for permission to reproduce copyright material:
Photo credits
Cover *l* © Bettmann/CORBIS, *r* akg-images; **p.8** SV-Bilderdienst/S.M.; **p.13** Mary Evans Picture Library; **p.14** *t* Bildarchiv Preussischer Kulturbesitz, *b* akg-images/ullstein bild; **p.18** akg-images; **p.23** akg-images; **p.24** *l* Ullstein-Archiv Gerstenberg, *r* Ullstein-Frentz; **p.25** Randall Bytwerk, German Propaganda Archive; **p.26** Randall Bytwerk, German Propaganda Archive; **p.27** *l* akg-images, *r* SV-Bilderdienst/Scherl; **p.28** Bildarchiv Preussischer Kulturbesitz, © The Heartfield Community of Heirs/VG Bild-Kunst,Bonn and DACS, London 2007; **p.29** SV-Bilderdienst/Scherl; **p.30** Mary Evans/Weimar Archive; **p.31** *l* Bildarchiv Preussischer Kulturbesitz, *r* Bildarchiv Preussischer Kulturbesitz, © DACS, London 2007; **p.32** Bildarchiv Preussischer Kulturbesitz; **p.33** *t* Topfoto, *b* Topfoto/Feltz; **p.34** *t* Topfoto/Alinari, *b* ullstein bild; **p.35** Reproduced by permission of Punch Ltd., www.punch.co.uk; **p.36** Randall Bytwerk, German Propaganda Archive; **p.38** Getty Images; **p.40** Topfoto; **p.41** *t* Stiftung Archiv der Akademie der Künste, Berlin (Photo: Roman März), © The Heartfield Community of Heirs/VG Bild-Kunst,Bonn and DACS, London 2007, *b* © Bettmann/Corbis; **p.43** akg-images; **p.44** © Bettmann/Corbis; **p.46** *t* David Low, Evening Standard, 3 July 1934, courtesy Evening Standard (photo: British Cartoon Archive, University of Kent), *b* Sidney George Strube, Daily Express, 3 July 1934, courtesy Express Newspapers (photo: British Cartoon Archive, University of Kent); **p.47** *t* Topfoto, *b* © Bettmann/Corbis; **p.49** Bildarchiv Preussischer Kulturbesitz; **p.51 & p.52** Randall Bytwerk, German Propaganda Archive; **p.53** Bildarchiv Preussischer Kulturbesitz; **p.54** SV-Bilderdienst/Scherl; **p.55** *l* Topfoto, *r* akg-images; **p.57** *l* akg-images, *r* Bundesarchiv Koblenz (Plak 003-011-012); **p.58** Bundesarchiv Berlin; **p.60** akg-images; **p.61** akg-images; **p.62** Mary Evans/Weimar Archive; **p.63** akg-images; **p.65** akg-images; **p.66** Getty Images; **p.68** akg-images; **p.69** Mary Evans/Weimar Archive; **p.70** Topfoto; **p.73** akg-images; **p.76** akg-images; **p.77** United States Holocaust Memorial Museum; **p.79** *l* Bundesarchiv Koblenz (Plak 003-002-046), *r* Bildarchiv Preussischer Kulturbesitz; **p.80** SV-Bilderdienst/Scherl; **p.82** Photo: The Wiener Library; **p.84** *l* ullstein bild, *r* Institut für Stadtgeschichte Frankfurt am Main; **p.85** akg-images; **p.86** SV-Bilderdienst/Scherl; **p.89** akg-images.

Acknowledgements
p.5 Edexcel Limited, *June 2006 Papers 1 and 2 1334 GCSE Modern World History*; **p.7** *A* P. Gay *Weimar Culture* (Pelican, 1974); **p.9** *B* E. Mowrer *Germany puts the clock back* (Penguin, 1937); **p.19** *A* K. Ludecke *I Knew Hitler* (Jarrolds, 1938); **p.20** *A* L. Snyder *The Weimar Republic* (Anvil Books, 1966); **p.21** *A* C. Bielenberg *The Past is Myself* (Chatto & Windus, 1968); **p.22** *A* H.H. Tiltman *Slump! A study of stricken Europe today* (Jarrolds, 1932); **p.30** *B* A. Speer *Inside the Third Reich* (Weidenfeld & Nicolson, 1970); **p.32** *B* I. Kershaw *Hitler 1889–1936: Hubris* (Allen Lane, 1998); **p.36** *A* J. Falter 'How likely were workers to vote for the NSDAP?', in *The Rise of Nationalism and the Working Classes in Weimar Germany*, ed. C. Fischer (Berghahn, 1996); **p.36** *B* C. Fischer *The Rise of the Nazis* (Manchester University Press, 1995); **p.38** *B* A. Speer *Inside the Third Reich* (Weidenfeld & Nicolson, 1970); **p.44** *B* H. Rauschning *Hitler Speaks* (Thornton Butterworth, 1940); **p.48** *C* J. Noakes & G. Pridham *Documents on Nazism 1919–45* (Cape, 1974); **p.49** *B* M. Bormann *Hitler's Table Talk* (Weidenfeld & Nicolson, 2000); **p.52** *B* K. Ludecke *I Knew Hitler* (Jarrolds, 1938); **p.65** *D* & **p.88** *F* J. Cloake *Nazi Germany* (Oxford University Press, 1997).

Every effort has been made to trace all copyright holders, but if any have been inadvertently overlooked the Publishers will be pleased to make the necessary arrangements at the first opportunity.

Although every effort has been made to ensure that website addresses are correct at time of going to press, Hodder Murray cannot be held responsible for the content of any website mentioned in this book. It is sometimes possible to find a relocated web page by typing in the address of the home page for a website in the URL window of your browser.

Hodder Headline's policy is to use papers that are natural, renewable and recyclable products and made from wood grown in sustainable forests. The logging and manufacturing processes are expected to conform to the environmental regulations of the country of origin.

Orders: please contact Bookpoint Ltd, 130 Milton Park, Abingdon, Oxon OX14 4SB. Telephone: +44 (0)1235 827720. Fax: +44 (0)1235 400454. Lines are open 9.00–5.00, Monday to Saturday, with a 24-hour message answering service. Visit our website at www.hoddereducation.co.uk.

© Steve Waugh and John Wright 2007
First published in 2007
by Hodder Murray, an imprint of Hodder Education,
a member of the Hodder Headline Group
338 Euston Road
London NW1 3BH

Impression number 5 4 3 2 1
Year 2010 2009 2008 2007

Typeset in 12 pt Garamond by Fakenham Photosetting Ltd, Fakenham, Norfolk
Artwork by: Richard Duszczak, Tony Jones, Tony Randell, Steve Smith
Printed in Italy

A catalogue record for this title is available from the British Library

ISBN: 978 0340 93976 5

Contents

Introduction

About the course

During this course you must study two outline studies, two depth studies and two coursework units. There are two written exam papers:

- In Paper 1 you have two hours to answer questions on two outline studies.
- In Paper 2 you have one and three quarter hours to answer questions on two depth studies.

About the book

This book is designed to help support the depth study 'Nazi Germany *c*.1930–39' and covers the key developments in Nazi Germany between 1930 and 1939. Throughout the study you will learn:

- why Adolf Hitler, who was a down-and-out before the First World War, became Chancellor of Germany in January 1933
- why there is still a mystery about the burning down of the German Parliament building in 1933
- what happened on the Night of the Long Knives
- how Hitler removed opposition in the years after 1933
- how a black American athlete called Jesse Owens threatened Hitler's racial theory
- what was meant by the Edelweiss Pirates
- what happened on the Night of the Broken Glass.

Each chapter in this book:

- contains activities – some help develop the historical skills you will need, others are exam-style questions which give you the opportunity to practise exam skills
- gives step-by-step guidance, model answers and advice on how to answer particular question types

- highlights glossary terms in bold the first time they appear.

About the depth studies (Paper 2)

Depth studies give you the opportunity to study a much shorter period in greater depth. As well as the depth study on Nazi Germany you will also study another one as part of this course. For example:

- The War to End Wars, 1914–1919
- Depression and the New Deal: The USA, 1929–1941
- The Russian Revolution, *c*.1910–1924
- The World at War, 1938–1945
- Conflict in Vietnam, 1963–1975
- The End of Apartheid in South Africa, 1982–1994

The depth studies are assessed through Paper 2. Paper 2 is a test of:

- knowledge and understanding of a shorter period in history
- the ability to answer four different types of source questions.

In order to answer Paper 2 questions successfully, you will need to have generic and question-specific source skills.

- 'Generic' means your ability to examine the nature, origins and purpose of sources.
- 'Question-specific' refers to the four different types of source questions. These are:
  - inference
  - cross-referencing
  - utility
  - synthesis (the ability to discuss an interpretation).

Depth study questions

In the examination you will be given six sources and have to answer four questions. Below are the questions (without the sources) on the depth study for the June 2006 exam.

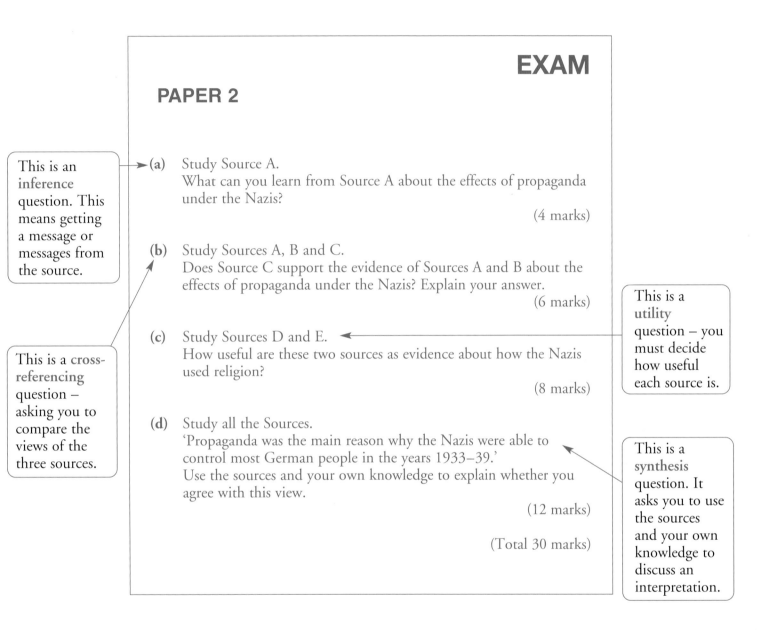

EXAM

PAPER 2

This is an **inference** question. This means getting a message or messages from the source.

(a) Study Source A.
What can you learn from Source A about the effects of propaganda under the Nazis?

(4 marks)

(b) Study Sources A, B and C.
Does Source C support the evidence of Sources A and B about the effects of propaganda under the Nazis? Explain your answer.

(6 marks)

This is a **cross-referencing** question – asking you to compare the views of the three sources.

This is a **utility** question – you must decide how useful each source is.

(c) Study Sources D and E.
How useful are these two sources as evidence about how the Nazis used religion?

(8 marks)

(d) Study all the Sources.
'Propaganda was the main reason why the Nazis were able to control most German people in the years 1933–39.'
Use the sources and your own knowledge to explain whether you agree with this view.

(12 marks)

(Total 30 marks)

This is a **synthesis** question. It asks you to use the sources and your own knowledge to discuss an interpretation.

You will be given step-by-step guidance on how to answer all these questions in the first five chapters. Chapter 6 will give the opportunity to practise all question types.

Generic source skills

Look at the four questions on the exam paper on the previous page. You will have to answer each of these four types of question for each of your depth studies in Paper 2. In order to answer these source questions you need to have some basic, general source skills. You need to be confident in examining the NOP of sources as this will help you to answer the questions set out later. This stands for:

Nature
Origin
Purpose

Examining the NOP of sources means asking:

Who?
When?
Why?
Where?
What?

Some examples of the type of question NOP encourages you to ask are given below.

Nature
• What type of source is it?

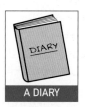
A DIARY

LETTER

PHOTOGRAPH

NEWSPAPER REPORT

SPEECH

CARTOON

• How will this influence the utility (usefulness) of the source? For example, photographs can capture only one moment in time but can still be useful.

Origin
• Who produced the source?
  – What do I know about this person or organisation?
  – Is this person or organisation likely to give a one-sided view of the event? If so, which side do I not get?

• When was the source produced?
  – Is it the evidence of an eyewitness? What are the advantages and disadvantages of eyewitness evidence?
  – Was it written at a later date? Did the person have the benefit of hindsight? What are the advantages and limitations of sources that were written later?
• Under what circumstances or in what situation was the source produced? For example, some sources are written under strict government control and **censorship** and the person who wrote the source may not have had the freedom to write what they genuinely believed.

Purpose
• Why was the source produced, written, drawn, etc?
• Is the source trying to make you support one view or one side? For example, cartoons are usually drawn to make fun of people and/or events.
• Is the source an example of propaganda? If so, what view is it trying to get across? (Be careful, propaganda sources are useful because they provide evidence of the methods used to gain support.)

This book will help to develop these generic source skills using a variety of sources and tasks.

1 Hitler and Nazism

Source A From *Weimar Culture* by the US historian P. Gay, written in 1974

The German people had had little practice in politics.... By 1919, there was democracy and the Weimar Republic opened the door to real politics, the Germans stood at the door, gaping, like peasants asked to a palace, hardly knowing how to behave themselves.

Task

Look at Source A. What message about politics in Germany is the author of Source A trying to put across?

On 9 November 1918, Kaiser Wilhelm II abdicated the German throne and fled to Holland. Germany became a republic and, two days later, the **armistice** was signed bringing an end to fighting in the Great War (1914–18). However, this did not signal peace for Germany and its citizens but merely ushered in a period of chaos and violence. The five years after the war saw an attempted Communist revolution, political assassinations, *Putsche* (armed uprisings) and massive inflation. Above all, Germans had to accept what they felt was a vindictive peace settlement – the Treaty of Versailles. Many Germans said that all the problems of the post-war years were the result of the decisions that had been made by the politicians of the new Weimar government.

This chapter answers the following questions:

• Why was the Weimar Republic unpopular before 1924?
• How did Adolf Hitler become involved in the Nazi Party?
• How did Hitler become leader of the party?
• Why did Hitler fail to achieve power in 1923?
• How did the Nazi Party change in the years 1924–29?

Source skills

In this chapter, you will look at the inference question from Paper 2. The question is worth four marks. There are also questions that help you develop an understanding of the topic. Do remember that in Paper 2, you have to answer questions which will not only focus on your source skills but also examine your knowledge and understanding of a topic.

Why was the Weimar Republic unpopular before 1924?

The ending of the war

The Great War had started in August 1914, and Europe was torn in two. Britain, France and Russia (the Allies) were ranged against Germany, Austria-Hungary and Turkey (the Central Powers). The USA joined the Allies in April 1917.

By the early autumn of 1918, the German army was being pushed back on the Western Front. Furthermore, the British naval blockade had imprisoned the German fleet at Kiel and caused grave shortages of food and vital war supplies. At the end of October 1918, the German navy mutinied and it was then that the German leaders realised they should seek peace. The armistice was signed on 11 November and there were many Germans who came to see the ending of the war as a betrayal of the German army. The notion was that the army had not been defeated by the Allies – it had been forced to surrender by the new government. The army had been 'stabbed in the back' (the *Dolchstoss*) by the politicians who signed the armistice. These politicians became known as the November Criminals.

The Communist threat

The new leader of Germany, Friedrich Ebert, then had to face the **Spartacist** uprising in Berlin in January 1919. The Spartacists were members of the **Communist Party** and they were attempting to overthrow the November Criminals and set up a Communist government. Ebert found that the *Reichswehr* (regular army) could not provide adequate forces to combat the Spartacists and he had to rely on the *Freikorps* to help restore order. The *Freikorps* were paramilitary groups made up of returning soldiers who refused to surrender weapons and were anti-Communist and anti-socialist. Together, the army and the *Freikorps* killed hundreds of **Communists** but there was so much violence that Ebert removed the government to the town of Weimar – hence the name of the new republic.

Ebert and the President, Philipp Scheidemann, were both members of the German **Social** Democratic Party (SPD) and, in order to retain power, they had relied on the army and had conspired in the deaths of many Communists. For some Germans this weakened the authority of the Weimar Republic.

Source A An election poster showing the *Dolchstoss*. This was published by the *Deutschnationale Volkspartei* (**DNVP**) in 1924. The poster is attacking the Social Democrats and says that if people vote for the SPD there will be another *Dolchstoss*. Such a vote would make Germans the slaves of Britain and France

Tasks

1. *Work in pairs. What can you learn from Source A about attitudes to the government? (This is an inference question. For further guidance see page 20.)*

2. *Find out why the Spartacists were given that name.*

The Weimar constitution

Following the abdication of the Kaiser, a new **constitution** had to be drawn up and this was finalised in August 1919. There were many flaws in the constitution and when things did not go well for Germany in the early post-war years, Ebert and his colleagues were criticised for creating a weak system of government.

The diagram on the right shows some of the flaws of the new constitution.

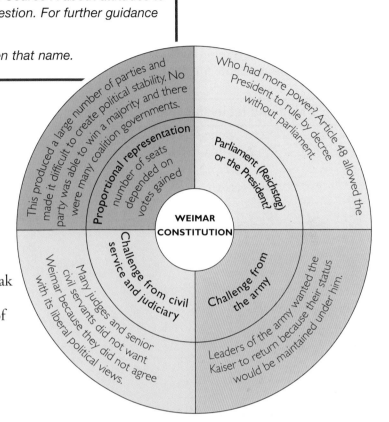

WEIMAR CONSTITUTION

Proportional representation — number of seats depended on votes gained. This produced a large number of parties and made it difficult to create political stability. No party was able to win a majority and there were many coalition governments.

Parliament (Reichstag) or the President? — Who had more power? Article 48 allowed the President to rule by decree without parliament.

Challenge from civil service and judiciary — Many judges and senior civil servants did not want Weimar because they did not agree with its liberal political views.

Challenge from the army — Leaders of the army wanted the Kaiser to return because their status would be maintained under him.

Source B Adapted from *Germany puts the clock back* by E. Mowrer, written in 1937. Mowrer was a **left-wing** American journalist

What can be said for a republic that allowed its laws to be interpreted by judges who supported the monarchy, its government to be run by people faithful to the old regime and then watched passively while teachers taught its children to despise the new system in favour of a glorified past? The Weimar Republic paid generous pensions to ex-officers and civil servants who were quite open in their desire to overthrow it.

Tasks

For all of these questions, work in pairs.

3. *Can you suggest reasons why many Germans accepted the idea of the 'stab in the back'?*

4. *Can you suggest reasons why the use of the army in 1919 'weakened the authority of the government'?*

5. *Look at the diagram above and Source B. What can you learn about the problems of the Weimar constitution? Here you need to consider how a country is run, for example, what part the army plays, what judges do, how a government is formed, who checks that there is smooth running of the country. It might be helpful to have a class discussion about this initially.*

6. *Place the problems of Weimar in order of their importance in weakening the government. Give reasons for your answer.*

The Treaty of Versailles

Although the Germans signed the armistice on 11 November 1918, it was not until 28 June 1919 that the treaty ending the war was signed. The Treaty of Versailles imposed extremely severe terms on Germany (see Source C) and most Germans felt that Ebert and the Weimar government were to blame for these.

Perhaps the harshest term for Germany was Article 231 – the War Guilt Clause. This stated that Germany had to accept blame for starting the war in 1914. For most Germans the Treaty stoked the fire of shame and humiliation. Versailles was nothing more than a dictated peace (*Diktat*). A **scapegoat** was needed – and the Weimar government and its politicians fitted the bill.

> **Source C Map and table showing some of the most important terms of the Treaty of Versailles**

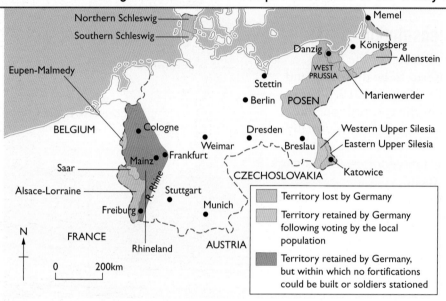

Territorial terms of the treaty of Versailles

Territorial terms	Military terms	Financial terms
All colonies to be given to the Allied Powers	Army not to exceed 100,000	Coal to be mined in the Saar by France
Alsace-Lorraine returned to France	No tanks, armoured cars and heavy artillery permitted	**Reparations** fixed at £6.6 billion
Eupen-Malmedy given to Belgium after a **plebiscite**	No military aircraft permitted	Cattle and sheep to be given to Belgium and France as reparations
Saar to be administered by the **League of Nations**	No naval vessel to be greater than 10,000 tons	Ships over 1,600 tons to be given up
Posen and West Prussia to Poland. Eastern Upper Silesia to Poland after a plebiscite	No submarines permitted	Germany to build merchant ships to replace Allied ships sunk by U-Boats
Danzig created a Free City		
Memel to be administered by the League of Nations		
No union (*Anschluss*) with Austria		
Northern Schleswig to Denmark after a plebiscite		
Rhineland demilitarised		

Source D An extract from a German newspaper, *Deutsche Zeitung*, 28 June 1919

Vengeance! German nation! Today in the Hall of Mirrors [Versailles] the disgraceful treaty is being signed. Do not forget it. The German people will, with unceasing work, press forward to reconquer the place among nations to which it is entitled. Then will come vengeance for the shame of 1919.

Source E A cartoon entitled 'Clemenceau the Vampire'. From the German right-wing satirical magazine, *Kladderadatsch*, published in July 1919. Clemenceau was the leader of France. The cartoon is commenting about the Treaty of Versailles

Tasks

7. *What can you learn from Source D about the impact of the Treaty of Versailles on Germany? (This is an inference question. For further guidance see page 20.)*

8. *Does Source E support the evidence of Sources D and C about the impact of the Treaty of Versailles on Germany? (This is a cross-referencing question. For further guidance, see pages 36–37.)*

9. *It is 1920. Write a letter to a newspaper, from the point of view of a German, explaining why you disagree with the terms of the Treaty of Versailles.*

Political unrest 1919–23

In its early years, the Weimar Republic faced constant threats from the left and right. The Communists were brutally put down in 1919 and 1920, and there were several other uprisings across Germany which threatened the existence of the government. The Berlin *Freikorps*, which had helped to crush the Communists, refused to disband and attempted to seize power. They failed. The French occupied the Ruhr again. The map shows the extent of unrest in Germany in the years to 1923. We shall read about Adolf Hitler's abortive Beer Hall *Putsch* on page 18.

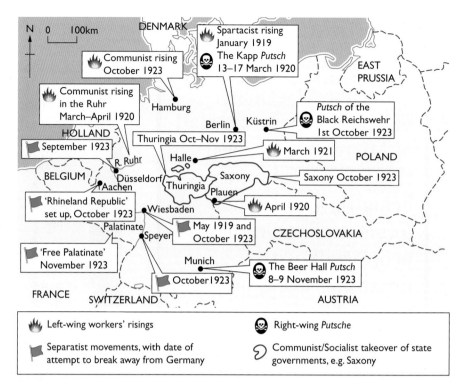

Political violence in Germany, 1919–23

Not only were there uprisings, but there were also many political assassinations carried out by ex-*Freikorps* members. There were 376 murders (354 of them were carried out by the right) in the period 1919–22. No right-wingers were sentenced to death but ten left-wingers were.

Economic instability

Germany had experienced inflation during the war and had borrowed extensively to finance the war effort. When the reparations figure was announced, the Weimar government claimed that it could not pay and, in 1921, began to print more money in order to pay France and Belgium as well as its own workers. The value of the German currency started to fall rapidly and, because no reparations were paid, France sent troops into the Ruhr, Germany's main industrial area. A further occupation took place in 1923 when Germany experienced **hyperinflation** as its currency lost all value. Those people with savings or those on a fixed income found themselves penniless. People were quick to blame the Weimar politicians.

Task

10. *What can you learn from the map about Germany in the years 1919–23? Explain your answer carefully.*

Source F Table showing the decreasing value of the mark against the pound, 1914–23	
July 1914	£1 = 20 marks
Jan 1919	£1 = 35 marks
Jan 1920	£1 = 256 marks
Jan 1921	£1 = 256 marks
Jan 1922	£1 = 764 marks
Jan 1923	£1 = 71,888 marks
July 1923	£1 = 1,413,648 marks
Sept 1923	£1 = 3,954,408,000 marks
Oct 1923	£1 = 1,010,408,000,000 marks
Nov 1923	£1 = 1,680,800,000,000,000 marks

However, in the summer of 1923, Gustav Stresemann became Chancellor and he began to steady things and introduced a new currency. The following year the new currency and loans from the USA enabled an economic recovery. It seemed as if the Weimar Republic had weathered the storms and could look forward to a period of stability and prosperity.

Tasks

11. Look at Source F.

    a) What can you learn about inflation in Germany in the years 1914–23?

    b) Why do you think pensioners and people who had savings in banks suffered more than most in the period of hyperinflation?

12. Look at Source G. In what ways does the cartoon help us to understand the problems of Germany in 1923?

13. Working in pairs, go over the problems faced by Germany after 1918 (pages 8–13). Which problem do you think was the most serious? Prepare a short case to present to the class to explain your choice.

14. Explain in no more than one sentence what you know about the following:

    - 'Stab in the back' theory
    - Diktat
    - November Criminals
    - Freikorps
    - Hyperinflation.

15. Design a concept map which shows either a reason why some Germans detested the Treaty of Versailles or a problem faced by Weimar after 1919.

Source G A cartoon published in Germany by the left-wing magazine *Simplicissimus* in 1923. The top caption reads 'Paper money' and the bottom one reads 'Bread'

How did Adolf Hitler become involved in the Nazi Party?

Task

1. *What can you learn from Source A about Hitler's political ideas in 1919? (This is an inference question. For further guidance, see page 20.)*

Biography Adolf Hitler 1889–1945

Early career

1889 Born at Braunau-am-Inn, Austria-Hungary

1903 Moved to live in Linz

1905 Moved to Vienna. Failed to secure place in the Academy of Arts

1907 Death of his mother

1913 Moved to Munich

1914 Enlisted in the German army

1916 Wounded at the Battle of the Somme

1918 Awarded the Iron Cross (First Class); wounded in a gas attack

Source B A painting of Hitler speaking to the National Socialist German Workers' Party in 1921

Hitler and the German Workers' Party

At the end of the First World War, Hitler was angry at the so-called defeat of Germany and hated the new Weimar Republic. He remained in the army and became an **informant** with its intelligence department in Munich. In September 1919, one of his duties was to attend and report on a meeting of the German Workers' Party (*Deutsche Arbeiter Partei*, **DAP**), a small group which had been founded by Anton Drexler in January of that year. At the meeting, Hitler was angered by the comments one of the speakers made and he made a powerful speech in reply. Drexler was so impressed by Hitler that he asked him to join the party and according to Hitler in *Mein Kampf* (Hitler's autobiography) he joined shortly afterwards. However, recent historical research has shown that Hitler was encouraged by his army superiors to join the party. Nevertheless, joining the party started Hitler on a political journey which saw him become the leader of Germany within fourteen years.

In the DAP, Hitler discovered that he was good at public speaking and his enthusiasm was soon rewarded within the party by being made responsible for recruitment and propaganda. He spoke at several meetings and his standard themes were:

The *Dolchstoss* (stab in the back)

Disgust at the Treaty of Versailles

Hatred of Weimar and the November Criminals

The Communist-Jewish conspiracy bent on destroying Germany

Tasks

2. *Look at Source B. What can you learn about Hitler from the source? (This is an inference question. For further guidance, see page 20.)*

3. *Look at the speech bubbles around Hitler's head on this page. Copy these and then add two or three sentences explaining why Hitler chose to speak about each one.*

How did Hitler become leader of the party?

In February 1920, Hitler and Drexler wrote what became known as the 25 Point Programme. It was a political **manifesto** and Hitler kept to most of the ideas throughout the rest of his life. The programme was announced at a key meeting in Munich and shortly after the words National Socialist were added to the party's name. The party grew rapidly in 1920 and Hitler was largely responsible for this – his public speaking attracted hundreds to meetings of the NSDAP.

Increased membership meant the party was able to buy up and publish its own newspaper – the *Völkischer Beobachter* (People's Observer). Hitler's influence on the party was such that he became its leader in mid-1921.

Key features of the 25 Point Programme

No. 1	The union of all Germans to form a Greater Germany.
No. 2	The scrapping of the Treaty of Versailles.
No. 4	Citizenship of the state to be granted only to people of German blood. Therefore no Jew was to be a citizen of the nation.
No. 6	The right to vote in elections to be allowed only to German citizens.
No. 7	Foreign nationals to be deported if it became impossible to feed the entire population.
No. 8	All non-Germans who entered the country after 1914 to leave.
No. 13	The government to **nationalise** all businesses that had been formed into corporations.
No. 14	The government to profit-share in major industries.
No. 17	An end to all speculation in land and any land needed for communal purposes would be seized. There would be no compensation.
No. 23	All newspaper editors and contributors to be German, and non-German papers to appear only with the permission of the government.
No. 24	Religious freedom for all – providing the views expressed did not threaten or offend the German people.
No. 25	The creation of a strong central government for the **Reich** to put the new programme into effect.

Tasks

1. *Study the 25 Point Programme above. Copy the table below and insert which parts of the programme relate to the particular area.*

Treaty of Versailles	Race	Religion	Civil rights	Industry

2. *Find out what the other points in the 25 Point Programme were and add them to your table.*

3. *Work in pairs. What does the 25 Point Programme show you about the ideology of the early Nazi Party?*

The early development of the Nazi Party

As leader of the Nazi Party, Hitler began to make some changes. He adopted the swastika (*der Hakenkreuz* – hooked cross) as the emblem of the party and the use of the raised arm salute. The political meetings in Munich at this time generated much violence and, in order to protect Nazi speakers, protection squads were used. These men were organised into the Gymnastic and Sports Section which was developed into the *Sturmabteilung* (**SA**) in 1921. The members of the SA were more commonly known as the 'Brownshirts' because of the colour of their uniform.

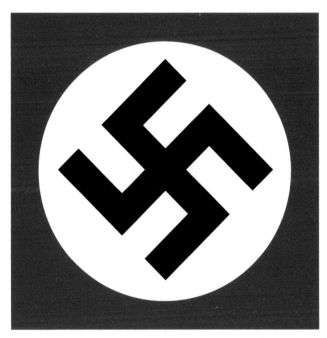

It is believed that Hitler chose to depict the swastika in a white circle on a red background because white stood for nationalism and red for the worker. The swastika was chosen possibly because it was anti-Semitic and stood for the victory of the Aryan man

The role of the *Sturmabteilung* (SA)

During the period 1921–23, the SA was used to disrupt the meetings of the Social Democratic and Communist Parties. Hitler ensured that there was maximum publicity for his party and membership grew from about 1,100 in June 1920 to about 55,000 in November 1923. Although at this point the Nazi Party was essentially a regional organisation with its main support in Bavaria, this did not stop Hitler having national political aims.

When the economic and political crises of 1923 hit Germany, Hitler decided that the Nazi Party was in a position to overthrow the regional government in Munich and could then march on Berlin.

> **Source A** The pledge of loyalty and obedience taken by members of the SA, the private army of the Nazi Party
>
> *As a member of the NSDAP, I pledge myself by its storm flag to:*
> - *be always ready to stake life and limb in the struggle for the aims of the movement*
> - *give absolute military obedience to my military superiors and leaders*
> - *bear myself honourably in and out of service.*

Tasks

4. *What can you learn from Source A about the SA? (This is an inference question. For further guidance see page 20.)*

5. *Working in groups, re-read the whole of this chapter. Then consider Hitler in 1923 – he was known only locally and he did not have a big army. Present a case for your class to explain why Hitler thought he and the Nazis would win national support in their bid to seize power in Germany.*

Why did Hitler fail to achieve power in 1923?

Hitler detested the Weimar Republic and, following the onset of hyperinflation and the invasion of the Ruhr by the French (see page 12), he felt that Weimar was now so disgraced it could easily be toppled. The Nazi Party had grown in strength and popularity in Munich and Bavaria, therefore, he decided his first step would be to seize control of Bavaria and then march on Berlin. He would then remove the weak Weimar politicians and form his own Nazi government.

On 8 November 1923, Hitler and 600 Nazis seized the Burgerbrau Keller (a huge beer hall which was often used for political meetings) in Munich. They captured the leader of the Bavarian government (von Kahr), the Chief of Police (von Seisser) and the head of the German army in Bavaria (von Lossow). Hitler won promises of support for his planned takeover from them after they had been held at gunpoint. This event is known as the Munich *Putsch*.

Seisser and Lossow changed their minds and the following day they organised troops and police to resist Hitler's planned armed march through Munich. The Nazis had only about 2,000 rifles and when they were challenged they were no match for the regular forces. Sixteen Nazis and three policemen were killed.

Hitler was arrested along with his main supporter General Ludendorff (Germany's leading general in the Great War and extremely popular across the country) and was tried for **treason**. The trial gave Hitler nationwide publicity and introduced him to the German public via the national press. He insisted that he was simply attempting to restore Germany's greatness and was resisting the weak and feeble Weimar government.

Hitler was found guilty of treason but the judges treated him leniently and sentenced him to five years in prison. He served only nine months and was released in December 1924. One other consequence of the *Putsch* was the banning of the Nazi Party.

Source A Hitler's announcement at the beginning of the Munich *Putsch* on 9 November 1923

Proclamation to the German people! The Government of the November Criminals in Berlin has today been deposed. A provisional [temporary] German National Government has been formed, this consists of General Ludendorff, Adolf Hitler and Colonel von Seisser.

Source B Armed SA men at a barricade in Munich, 9 November 1923. The future leader of the SS, Heinrich Himmler, is holding the pre-1918 German flag in the middle of the photograph

Tasks

1. *Look at Source A. Can you suggest reasons why some Germans might have supported Hitler in the* Putsch?

2. *Can you suggest reasons why it was important for Hitler to have Colonel von Seisser on the side of the Nazis in the* Putsch?

3. *Why do you think that Hitler received such a lenient sentence? (Look back to pages 8 and 12.)*

4. *Look at Source B. Can you suggest why the flag is of such importance to the Nazis?*

How did the Nazi Party change in the years 1924–29?

During his nine months in Landsberg prison, Hitler completed his autobiography *Mein Kampf* (My Struggle) which contained his political views.

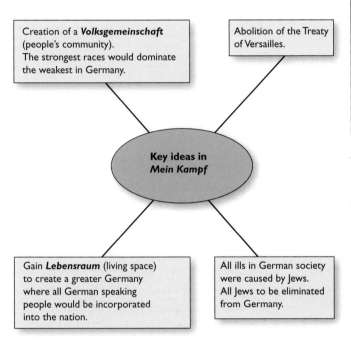

Creation of a *Volksgemeinschaft* (people's community). The strongest races would dominate the weakest in Germany.

Abolition of the Treaty of Versailles.

Key ideas in *Mein Kampf*

Gain *Lebensraum* (living space) to create a greater Germany where all German speaking people would be incorporated into the nation.

All ills in German society were caused by Jews. All Jews to be eliminated from Germany.

Task

1. *Design an advertisement for* Mein Kampf. *Focus on why it is important for Germans to read, how it shows Hitler's ideas and how it will change people's political opinions.*

The fortunes of the party declined when Hitler was in prison. The replacement leader, Alfred Rosenberg, had few leadership qualities and in the elections of 1924, the Nazis lost votes. Shortly after his release from prison, the Nazi Party was re-launched and Hitler slowly began to take control once again. It was decided to create party branches, called *Gaue*, across Germany; each was to be led by a *Gauleiter*.

Source A Comments made by Hitler as a prisoner in Landsberg. He was speaking to a fellow Nazi inmate

When I resume active work, it will be necessary to follow a new policy. Instead of working to achieve power by armed conspiracy, we shall have to hold our noses and enter parliament against the Catholic and Communist members. If out-voting them takes longer than out-shooting them, at least the results will be guaranteed by their own Constitution. Sooner or later, we shall have a majority in parliament....

At the Bamberg party conference in 1926, further changes were made to the party organisation. Possible rivals such as Josef Goebbels and Gregor Strasser were won over. Hitler was the undisputed leader and his message was to use endless propaganda to win over the voters. The 25 Point Programme of 1920 was accepted, however in 1928 Point 17 (see page 16) was amended to say that privately owned land would only be confiscated if it was owned by a Jew. Hitler had tried to win the support of the urban voters but, in 1928, he decided that the rural voters should be targeted. This came at a time when farmers began to experience economic problems and found Nazism attractive.

Yet, despite the changes, the Nazis won only twelve seats in parliament in the 1928 elections. There were further reforms to the party in 1929 and political and economic events that year helped the Nazi Party rise from relative obscurity to become one of the leading parties in the country.

Tasks

2. *What can you learn from Source A about Hitler's view on politics? (This is an inference question. For further guidance see page 20.)*

3. *Explain why the Bamberg Conference was important for Hitler.*

4. *Why do you think Point 17 was altered?*

Examination practice

The people who were wiped out lost all sense of security. Widows, civil servants, teachers, army officers and pensioners lost their lifetime savings. It was the scar that never healed. These were the people who turned to Hitler to lead them out of chaos.

My critical faculty was swept away. Leaning forward as if he were trying to force his inner self into the consciousness of all these thousands, he was holding the masses, and me with them, under a hypnotic spell by the sheer force of his belief... I forgot everything but the man; then glancing around, I saw that his magnetism was holding these thousands as one.

Question 1 – inference

What can you learn from Source A about the impact of hyperinflation? (4 marks)

How to answer

This is an inference question. You are being asked to give the message or messages of the source, to read between the lines of what is written. For example, in Source A there are several messages.

Question 2 – inference

What can you learn from Source B about Hitler's public speaking powers? (4 marks)

Now have a go yourself

- Begin your answer with 'This source suggests...'. This should help you get a message or messages from the source.
- Avoid repeating the content.
- Look for key words in the source that might lead to inferences.
- You could tackle this by copying the source and highlighting different messages in different colours to help identify messages like those in Question 1.

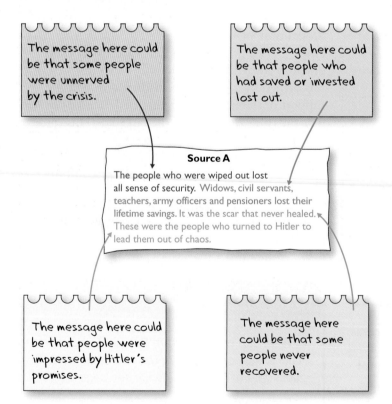

The message here could be that some people were unnerved by the crisis.

The message here could be that people who had saved or invested lost out.

Source A

The people who were wiped out lost all sense of security. Widows, civil servants, teachers, army officers and pensioners lost their lifetime savings. It was the scar that never healed. These were the people who turned to Hitler to lead them out of chaos.

The message here could be that people were impressed by Hitler's promises.

The message here could be that some people never recovered.

The overall message could be that hyperinflation hit many middle-class people and that hyperinflation was a key factor in the rise of Hitler.

2 The Nazi rise to power 1929–33

Source A From *The Past is Myself* written in 1968 by Christabel Bielenberg, an Englishwoman who lived in Germany under the Nazis. Here, she is remembering a conversation with Herr Neisse, her gardener

Then came 1929 and economic trouble, and a huge wave rolled over Europe and America leaving a trail of bankruptcies. Herr Neisse lost the chance to own a vegetable stall and he lost his job. He joined an army of six million unemployed... Communism did not appeal to him... he just wanted to belong somewhere. National Socialism was more like it. He began to go to Nazi Party meetings... he was told that the Jews were the evil root of all Germany's problems. Although he knew of the corruption of party members he believed Hitler knew nothing of it. Neisse said 'Hitler loves children and dogs too.'

Task

What can you learn from Source A about the attractions of the Nazi Party after 1929? (Remember how to answer this type of question? For further guidance, see page 20.)

In the period 1929–33, the Nazis became the largest political party in Germany. Hitler was able to appeal to all classes of society; his simple messages and slogans could be understood by all. The Depression of the early 1930s suited the Nazi Party and by January 1933, Hitler had become the Chancellor of Germany. He had fulfilled the promise he made when he was released from Landsberg jail – he had become leader through the ballot box.

   This chapter answers the following questions:

• What was the impact of the Great Depression on Germany?
• What methods did the Nazi Party use to increase its support?
• What was the role of Hitler in increasing support for the Nazis?
• How did the events of July 1932–January 1933 bring Hitler to power?

Source skills
This chapter reinforces some of the inference skills from Chapter 1. It also gives guidance on the Paper 2 cross-referencing question. This is worth six marks.

What was the impact of the Great Depression on Germany?

Task

1. *Study Source A. What do you think the writer means when he says 'politics have become a matter of bread and butter'?*

By 1929, Germany had experienced five years of prosperity. The loans from the USA had helped to remove inflation and there had been much investment in industry. However, the prosperity depended on the USA and when its stock market collapsed in October 1929, the problems created there had huge consequences for the German economy. The death of Stresemann added to the crisis. It was felt that he was the only person who would be able to steer Germany through troubled times again.

Bankers and financiers in the USA now recalled the loans made under the **Dawes Plan** to Germany in 1924. International trade began to contract and German exports fell rapidly in the years after 1929. The **Great Depression** had arrived in Germany. Unemployment began to rise as employers sacked workers and factories closed. German farmers had already been experiencing problems and the continued fall in food prices worsened their plight.

Unemployment continued to rise in the early 1930s and by mid-1932 the total exceeded 6 million. This meant that four out of every ten German workers were without jobs. Unlike 1923, the fear in Germany this time was not inflation, it was unemployment. If a political party could offer clear and simple solutions to the economic problems, it would readily win votes. The workers wanted jobs and the middle classes wanted to avoid a Communist revolution.

Source B Chart showing German industrial production, 1929–33

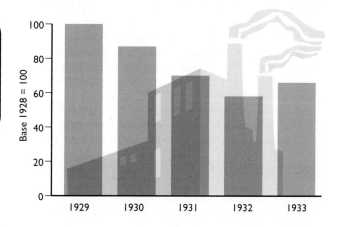

Source C Graph showing unemployment in Germany, 1928–32

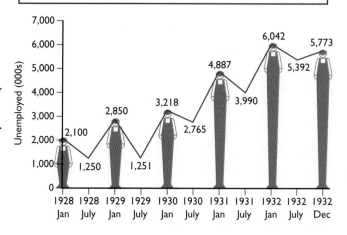

Source D Unemployed men in Hanover, 1930

The economic crisis created problems for the Weimar government and there was little agreement about how to tackle unemployment and poverty. In early 1930, some of Chancellor Brüning's proposals were rejected by the Socialist Party and the **coalition government** broke up. Brüning remained as Chancellor but was unable to secure a majority of members to carry out his policies. He therefore had to rely on President Hindenburg to use **decrees**. From this point, the *Reichstag* (parliament) was used less frequently and democracy was challenged.

Source E The role of the *Reichstag* and the President, 1930–32

	1930	1931	1932
Presidential decrees	5	44	66
***Reichstag* laws**	98	34	5
***Reichstag*: days sitting**	94	42	13

Because Brüning did not have a majority in the *Reichstag*, he called a general election in September 1930. It was this election that gave the Nazis their breakthrough. They won 107 seats and became the second biggest party in Germany after the **Social Democrats** (SPD) who won 143. Brüning could still not rely on having his policies accepted in the *Reichstag* and he came to depend more and more on President Hindenburg (see Source E). Another crisis arose when Brüning proposed to break up large agricultural estates in East Prussia. This was opposed by landowners and Hindenburg refused to pass the decree.

Brüning resigned in May 1932. His time as Chancellor had seen the Nazis have successes in the regional and general elections. Moreover, during the next eight months there was continued political and economic turmoil which saw the extreme parties become more violent. The Depression seemed to have unleashed chaos across Germany.

Tasks

2. *Study Sources B and C. What can you learn from these sources about the impact of the Depression on Germany in the years to 1933? (Remember how to answer this type of question? For further guidance see page 20.)*

3. *Does Source D support the evidence of Sources B and C about the impact of the Depression on Germany? Explain your answer. (This is a cross-referencing question. For further guidance see pages 36–37.)*

4. *Look closely at the men in Source D. What do you notice about them? Look at their appearance and expressions.*

5. *Work as a group of three or four. Imagine you are setting up a political party in Germany in 1930. Make a list of the key points you would raise in order to appeal to German citizens and win their vote. Design posters to show your political beliefs.*

6. *Study Source E. What does this source show about democracy in Weimar Germany in the years 1930–32?*

What methods did the Nazi Party use to increase its support?

The role of Josef Goebbels

During the years 1929–33, the Nazis increased their support through propaganda. They did this in a variety of ways such as having mass rallies, putting up posters in prominent places and displaying banners wherever possible so that the Nazis appeared to be everywhere.

The Nazis were most fortunate in having a person who understood how to use the mass media and also manipulate huge audiences. Josef Goebbels ensured that the Nazi message was simple and frequently repeated. By the early 1930s, the Nazis had 120 daily or weekly newspapers regularly read by hundreds of thousands of people across the country. As Germany descended into political chaos in 1930–32, Goebbels was able to present the Nazi Party in local, regional, national and presidential elections. The Nazi message was heard everywhere, especially on the radio.

> Source A Nazi Party election poster, 1930. The words at the top read: 'List 9 National Socialist German Workers' Party'. Some of the words coming from the snake are: money-lending, Versailles, unemployment, war, guilt, lie, **Bolshevism**, inflation and terror.

Biography Josef Goebbels 1897–1945

Early career

1897 Born in Rheydt in the Rhineland

1921 Left Heidelberg University gaining a PhD in literature and philosophy

1922 (or 1924) Joined the Nazi Party

1927 Set up his own newspaper *Der Angriff* (The Attack)

1928 Elected to the *Reichstag*

1929 Appointed Head of Propaganda of the Nazi Party

1933 Appointed Minister for Propaganda and Popular Enlightenment

Nazi electoral success

As you have seen on page 23, the Nazis won 107 seats in the 1930 general election having won only twelve in 1928. Furthermore, they continued to win support in the regional elections. They were undoubtedly helped in their electoral success by the Great Depression. The Nazi message was that Weimar had caused the economic crisis and the weak coalition governments had no real solutions to offer. The Nazis alone could unite Germany in a time of economic crisis.

The Nazis then played on the resentment of the Treaty of Versailles. The old wounds were re-opened and Germany's problems were blamed on the November Criminals and the Weimar Republic. Only the Nazis could restore Germany to its former glory.

If there were any who doubted the simple Nazi messages, then Hitler ensured that another scapegoat could be offered. He blamed the Jews for Germany's problems saying:

- they were involved not only with Communism but also the evils of **capitalism**
- they had helped to cause unemployment
- they had conspired in Germany's defeat in the Great War
- they had been involved in the Bolshevik Revolution
- they were preparing to cause a revolution in Germany which would mean that all private property and wealth would be seized by the state.

Source B Nazi election poster, 1932. The text reads 'Work and bread'. The poster shows all kinds of tools being given out showing that the Nazis would help all kinds of workers.

Source C An extract from *Mein Kampf*, Hitler's autobiography

Propaganda must confine itself to a very few points and repeat them endlessly. Here, as with so many things in this world, persistence is the first and foremost condition of success.

The presidential election 1932: the campaign

During the presidential election of 1932, when Hitler stood against Hindenburg, the Nazis were quick to use modern technology. For example, by using the aeroplane Hitler was able to speak at as many as five cities on the same day, flying from one venue to the next. Goebbels ensured that there were mass rallies and that not only was the Nazi message being spread, but also Hitler was being recognised as a national political figure. The message was put over in films, on the radio and even records. Goebbels mastered the art of propaganda in these years. President Hindenburg did not campaign.

> **Source D** The cover of the book *Hitler über Deutschland* (Hitler over Germany), published in Germany in 1932

The presidential election 1932: the results

Hindenburg only just failed to win more than 50 per cent of the votes in the election and so there had to be a second round. Hitler was quite successful in winning a large number of votes in each round, though he was quite disappointed at his showing.

Candidate	First round	Second round
Hindenburg	18,650,000	19,360,000
Hitler (NSDAP)	11,340,000	13,420,000
Thälmann (KPD)	4,968,000	3,710,000

Results of the presidential election: first round, March 1932 and second round, April 1932

The tactics used by Hitler and Goebbels were paying off and there was greater success in the *Reichstag* elections in July 1932 (see page 29). Goebbels ensured that the German people were given positive images of Hitler and the Nazis. He also played on their fears.

Task

4. *Does Source G support the evidence of Sources E and F about the reasons people voted for Hitler? (This is a cross-referencing question. For further guidance see pages 36–37.)*

Source E A Nazi election poster of 1932. It says: 'Our last hope – Hitler'

Source F A Nazi poster of 1932. It says 'We farmers are getting rid of the dung' and 'We are voting Nazi'. The dung represents Jews and Socialists

Source G From a Nazi election leaflet of 1932

The German farmer stands in between two great dangers today – one is the American capitalist system and the other is the Marxist economic system of BOLSHEVISM. Capitalism and Bolshevism work hand in hand; they are born of Jewish thought and serve the master plan of Jews all over the world. Who alone can save the farmer from these dangers?

NATIONAL SOCIALISM

Task

5. *Re-read pages 21–27, then look at the table below. Complete the boxes, giving at least one reason why the Nazis could appeal to each group. Your finished table will show how the Nazis could appeal to different groups of society at the same time.*

Social group	How Nazis could appeal to them
Working classes	
Farmers	
Middle classes	
Upper classes	

Financial support for the Nazis

Hitler and the Nazis could not have conducted their campaigns without financial backers. One example of how funds were crucial came in 1932, when 600,000 copies of the Nazi economic programme were produced and distributed in the July *Reichstag* election. The Nazi Party received funds from leading industrialists such as Thyssen, Krupp and Bosch. These industrialists were terrified of the Communist threat and were also concerned at the growth of **trade union** power. They knew that Hitler reviled Communism and that he would reduce the influence of the unions.

Furthermore, by 1932, the Nazis had begun to develop close links with the National Party (**DNVP**). The DNVP leader, Alfred Hugenberg, was a newspaper tycoon, and permitted the Nazis to publish articles which attacked Chancellor Brüning. Hence, Goebbels was able to continue the nationwide campaign against Weimar and keep the Nazis in the forefront of people's minds.

In his speeches, Hitler claimed that parliamentary democracy did not work and said that only he and the NSDAP could provide the strong government that Germany needed. The Nazis used the SA (see page 17) not only to provide protection for their meetings but also to disrupt the meetings of their opponents, especially the Communists. The Communists had their own private army *die Rotfrontkämpfer* (Red Front fighters) and there were countless fights between the two. On many occasions, there were fatalities. Hitler sought to show the German people that he could stamp out the Bolshevik violence and their threat of revolution.

Source H An anti-Hitler poster by a Communist, John Heartfield. Born Helmut Herzfeld, he changed his name as a protest against the Nazis. He fled Germany in 1933. The caption reads 'The meaning of the Hitler salute. Motto: millions stand behind me! Little man asks for big gifts'

DER SINN DES
HITLERGRUSSES:

Motto:
MILLIONEN
STEHEN
HINTER MIR!

Kleiner Mann bittet um große Gaben

Source I Results of the July 1932 General Election		
Political party	**Number of *Reichstag* seats**	**% of vote**
Nazis (NSDAP)	230	37.4%
Social Democrats	133	21.6%
Communist Party (KPD)	89	14.3%
Centre Party (ZP)	75	12.5%
National Party (DNVP)	37	5.9%
People's Party (DVP)	7	1.2%
Democratic Party (DDP)	4	1.0%

Tasks

6. *Study Source H. What can you learn about support for Hitler in the 1930s? (Remember how to answer this type of question? For further guidance see page 20.)*

7. *How useful is Source H as evidence of the support for Hitler and the Nazis? (This is a utility question. For further guidance see pages 51 and 59–61.)*

8. *Look at Source J. Explain why it was important for Hitler to have the SA involved in battles with the Communists.*

Source J A battle between SA members and Communist Front Fighters in 1932. The signs read: 'Up the Revolution' and 'Free the political prisoners'

What was the role of Hitler in increasing support for the Nazis?

Source A Part of a speech made by Hitler in Munich, August 1923

The day must come when a German government will summon up the courage to say to the foreign powers:

'The Treaty of Versailles is founded on a monstrous lie. We refuse to carry out its terms any longer. Do what you will! If you want war, go and get it! Then we shall see if you can turn 70 million Germans into slaves!'

Either Germany sinks. . . or else we dare to enter on the fight against death and the devil. . . .

Task

1. *What can you learn about Hitler from Source A? (Remember how to answer this type of question? For further guidance see page 20.)*

As you read on pages 15–16, Hitler quickly developed the art of public speaking and his speeches did attract many people and helped increase the membership of the Nazi Party. He helped to draw up the 25 Point Programme (see page 16) and he was fully aware that after the *Putsch* he had to present himself and his party as law-abiding and democratic. He also knew that he had to be able to offer something to all groups in German society if he was to be successful in any elections.

Source B Nazi Party rally in Nuremberg, 1927

Source C From *Inside the Third Reich* by Albert Speer, written in 1970. Speer was recalling a meeting in Berlin in 1930 at which Hitler spoke. Speer was a university lecturer and later became Minister of Armaments in Nazi Germany

I was carried away on a wave of enthusiasm [by the speech]... the speech swept away any scepticism, any reservations. Opponents were given no chance to speak... Here, it seemed to me, was hope. Here were new ideals, a new understanding, new tasks. The peril of Communism, which seemed inevitably on its way, could be stopped. Hitler persuaded us that, instead of hopeless unemployment, Germany could move to economic recovery.

Source D Adapted from the diary of Luise Solmitz, 23 March 1932. A schoolteacher, Solmitz was writing about attending a meeting in Hamburg at which Hitler spoke.

There stood Hitler in a simple black coat, looking over the crowd of 120,000 people of all classes and ages... a forest of swastika flags unfurled, the joy of this moment showed itself in a roaring salute... The crowd looked up to Hitler with touching faith, as their helper, their saviour, their deliverer from unbearable distress... He is the rescuer of the scholar, the farmer, the worker and the unemployed.

Source E A photo taken to show Hitler's love of children.

Hitler could be all things to all people. He was the war hero, the saviour and also the ordinary man in the street. The image created was that his whole existence was given over to Germany and there were no distractions to prevent him achieving his goals. He had created a philosophy which all could comprehend and furthermore, his vision of the future revolved around making Germany the strongest nation in the world. Hitler had the one characteristic that most other politicians lacked – charisma.

Source F An official painting of Hitler by Franz Triebsch

Tasks

2. *Study Sources B, C and D. Does Source D support the evidence of Sources B and C about Hitler's attraction? Explain your answer. (This is a cross-referencing question. For further guidance see pages 36–37.)*

3. *Study Sources E and F. How useful is each source in helping you understand how Hitler was portrayed? (This is a utility question. For further guidance see pages 51 and 59–61.)*

How did the events of July 1932–January 1933 bring Hitler to power?

Source A Ernst Thälmann, leader of the German Communist Party, speaking at an open-air meeting in Berlin, 1932

Task

1. *What can you learn from Source A about the German Communist Party at this time? (Remember how to answer this type of question? For further guidance see page 20.)*

You have already seen that Hitler was quite successful in the presidential elections in March and April 1932. He was by now the leader of the second largest party in the *Reichstag* and he was well known across Germany. When a general election was called for 31 July 1932, the Nazis were optimistic about improving on the number of votes they had won in the previous election of September 1930.

There was much violence in the run up to the election. About 100 people were killed and more than 1,125 wounded in clashes between the political parties. On 17 July there were at least 19 people killed in Hamburg.

More people voted in July than in any previous Weimar election. The Nazis won 230 seats and were now the largest party in the *Reichstag* (see Source I, page 29). However, Chancellor von Papen of the **Centre Party**, despite not having the most seats, did not relinquish his post and began to scheme with President Hindenburg. Hitler demanded the post of Chancellor and at a meeting with Hitler in August, Hindenburg refused to contemplate Hitler even if he did lead the largest party in the *Reichstag*.

Source B From *Adolf Hitler* by I. Kershaw, written in 1998

At the meeting in August, Hindenburg refused Hitler the Chancellorship. He could not answer, he said, before God, his conscience and the Fatherland if he handed over entire the power of the government to a single party and one which was so intolerant towards those with different views.

Task

2. Study Source B. What can you learn from Source B about Hindenburg's attitude to the Nazi Party? (Remember how to answer this type of question? For further guidance see page 20.)

It was not possible for any party to command a majority in the *Reichstag* and it was impossible to maintain a coalition. Von Papen dissolved the *Reichstag* in September and new elections were set for early November. Von Papen held the opinion that the Nazis were losing momentum and if he held on, they would slowly disappear from the scene. He was correct about them losing momentum as the results of the election showed.

Source C November 1932 election results

Political party	Number of *Reichstag* seats	% of vote
Nazis (NSDAP)	196	33.1%
Social Democrats	121	20.4%
Communist Party (KPD)	100	16.9%
Centre Party (ZP)	70	11.9%
National Party (DNVP)	52	8.8%
People's Party (DVP)	11	1.9%
Democratic Party (DDP)	2	1.0%

Task

3. Compare the results of the July and November 1932 elections in Source C. For the results of the July elections see Source I on page 29. Can you suggest reasons why the parties experienced differing fortunes?

Biography Franz von Papen 1879–1969

Career to 1933
1879 Born in Werl, Westphalia
1913 Entered the diplomatic service as a military attaché to the German ambassador in Washington DC
1917 German army adviser to Turkey and also served as a major in the Turkish army in Palestine
1918 Left the German army in 1918. Entered politics and joined the Catholic Centre Party
1922 Elected to the *Reichstag*
1932 Appointed Chancellor, schemed with Hindenburg thinking Hitler and the Nazis could be manipulated
1933 Appointed Vice-Chancellor under Hitler. Assumed Hitler could be dominated

Biography Paul von Hindenburg 1846–1934

1846 Born in Posen
1866 Joined the Prussian army
1870–71 Fought in the Franco-Prussian War
1903 Reached the rank of general
1914 Commanded German armies in East Prussia. Victorious at the Battles of Tannenberg and Masurian Lakes
1916 Made Chief of General Staff
1918 Retired from the army
1919 Put forward the *Dolchstoss* theory (see page 8)
1925–34 President of Germany

Chapter 2 The Nazi rise to power 1929–33 (33)

Political intrigue

However, von Papen could not secure a majority in the *Reichstag* and, at the same time, Hitler continued to demand the post of Chancellor. Von Papen suggested abolishing the Weimar constitution and at this, Kurt von Schleicher, the Minister of Defence, persuaded Hindenburg that if this happened there might be civil war. Von Papen lost Hindenburg's confidence and resigned. He was succeeded by Schleicher, who hoped to attain a majority in the *Reichstag* by forming a so-called *Querfront*, meaning 'cross-front', whereby he would bring together different strands from left and right parties.

Von Papen was determined to regain power and to this end he met Hitler in early January 1933 and it was decided that Hitler should lead a **Nazi-Nationalist government** with von Papen as the Vice-Chancellor. Intrigue and chicanery now took the place of considered open political debate. The army, major landowners and leaders of industry were convinced that von Papen and Hitler were saving Germany from Schleicher's plans and a possible Communist takeover. Von Papen was able to convince President Hindenburg that a coalition government with Hitler as Chancellor would save Germany and bring stability to the country. Von Papen said that he would be able to control Hitler – he would 'make Hitler squeak'.

On 30 January 1933, Adolf Hitler became Chancellor of Germany. He was the leader of the largest party and he had been invited to be leader by the President. He had achieved his aim of becoming Chancellor by legal and democratic means.

Source D Hitler accepting the chancellorship from President Hindenburg in 1933

Biography Kurt von Schleicher 1882–1934

1882 Born in Brandenburg
1900 Joined German army
1914–18 Staff Officer to Hindenburg
1919 Organised *Freikorps*
1925 Political adviser to Hindenburg
1932 Appointed Chancellor
1934 Murdered in the Night of the Long Knives (see pages 44–45)
(Some of the many translations of the German word *Schleicher* are – sneaky, furtive, intriguer)

THE TEMPORARY TRIANGLE.

VON HINDENBURG AND VON PAPEN (*together*)—
"FOR HE'S A JOLLY GOOD FELLOW,
FOR HE'S A JOLLY GOOD FELLOW,
FOR HE'S A JOLLY GOOD FE-EL-LOW,
(*Aside:* "Confound him!")
AND SO SAY BOTH OF US!"

Tasks

4. Look at Source E. What do you think is meant by the term 'temporary triangle'?

5. Re-read pages 32–35, looking carefully at Sources A–E. The events of 1932 are complex. To simplify things, complete the table below. In each box write the main actions of the individual from mid-1932 to 1933.

Hitler	von Papen	von Schleicher	Hindenburg

6. Place the events in chronological order, beginning January 1932 and going up to January 1933.

Examination practice

The second question on Paper 2 asks you to cross-reference three sources.

Source A From a book about the voting patterns of Germans in the Weimar Republic

According to estimates, probably one in three workers of voting age backed the NSDAP. In July 1932 more workers would have voted NSDAP than KPD or SPD. On a regular basis over a quarter of National Socialist voters were workers. There is unmistakable over-representation of voters from the middle classes.

Source C From a book about the rise of the Nazis

The Nazis enjoyed a degree of success in crossing class, regional and gender barriers. It does appear that by 1932 about 40 per cent of voters and party members were working class as were some 60 per cent of the SA. The Nazis did have successes in Protestant agricultural areas.

Question 1 – cross-referencing

Does Source C support the evidence of Sources A and B about support for the Nazi Party? Explain your answer. (6 marks)

Source B A Nazi election poster from 1932. The words read 'Work and bread from National Socialism'

How to answer

- Examine Sources A and C. Make a note of any part of Source C that shows support for Source A. There may be no support.
- Now explain any areas of support between the two sources.

Example:
Source C supports Source A in mentioning that many workers voted for the NSDAP. Source C mentions that about 40 per cent of voters were working class as were 60 per cent of the SA members.

- Make a note of any part of Source C that does not support Source A. There may be no differences.
- Now explain any differences between the two sources.

Example:
Source C says it was 40 per cent working class support yet in Source A it mentions 1 in 3 for such support and fewer regularly supporting the NSDAP.

- Now make a judgement on how much C supports A. Use judgement words or phrases such as 'there is strong support', 'there is little support', 'strongly agree' or 'very little agreement'.

Example:
For the most part Source C agrees with Source A about the support but it is the actual figures which vary.

- Examine Sources B and C. Make a note of any part of Source C that shows support for B. There may be no support.
- Now explain any areas of support between the two sources.

Example:
Source C supports Source B because both mention the workers. Source B is appealing to the workers to vote for the Nazi Party and C mentions that the Nazis had workers' support in 1932.

- Make a note of any part of Source C that does not support Source B. There may be no differences to highlight.
- Now explain any differences between the two sources.

Example:
However, Source C gives figures and Source B is an appeal to workers and there is no mention of other groups.

- Now make a judgement on how much C supports B. Use judgement words or phrases such as 'there is strong support', 'there is little support', 'strongly agree' or 'very little agreement'.

Example:
To a degree, there is some support as both do focus on workers' support.

- Finally write a conclusion. Begin with the word 'overall'.
- Make a judgement on how much support there is between C and each of the other two sources. Remember to use judgement words/phrases.

Example:
Overall Source C agrees quite strongly with Source A, especially about the number of supporters but there are some discrepancies. However, support is less strong in B because there are no figures, just an appeal. Though C and A agree about other classes, no mention is made in B.

Question 2 – cross-referencing

Now have a go yourself
Does Source C support the evidence of Sources A and B about the appeal of the Nazis? (6 marks)

Source A Nazi election poster. It says 'Workers – choose the soldier at the front – Hitler'

ARBEITER

WÄHLT DEN FRONTSOLDATEN

HITLER!

Source B From the memoirs of Albert Speer, 1970. Speer was the Nazi Minister for Armaments and a close adviser to Hitler

It must have been in 1930 or 1931 that my mother saw an SA parade in the streets of Heidelberg. The sight of discipline in a time of chaos, the impression of energy in an atmosphere of universal hopelessness, seem to have won her over. At any rate, without ever having heard a speech or read a pamphlet, she joined the party.

Source C From an article in the *Munich Observer*, March 1932

Hitler is the password of all who believe in Germany's re-birth. Hitler is the last hope of those who were deprived of everything: of farm and home, of savings, of a job and survival. Hitler is the word of deliverance for millions, for they are in despair.

3 The creation of the Nazi state

Source A An extract from Hitler's 'Appeal to the German people' made on 31 January 1933, the day after he had been appointed Chancellor of Germany

In the last fourteen years the November parties have created an army of millions of unemployed. Germany must not and will not sink into Communist anarchy... We have unbounded confidence, for we believe in our nation and in its eternal values... In place of our turbulent instincts, the new government will make national discipline govern our life... We do not recognise classes, only the German people with its millions of farmers, citizens and workers who together will either overcome this distress or give in to it. Now, German people give us four years and then judge us.

Task

Study Source A. What can you learn from this source about Hitler's intentions? (Remember how to answer this type of question? For further guidance see page 20.)

In the period January 1933 to August 1934, Hitler and the Nazis secured control of all aspects of the German state. By August 1934, Hitler had combined the posts of Chancellor and President and was safe in the knowledge that the army supported him. Moreover, the banning of political parties, the control of the media, trade unions and police ensured that there was little or no opposition to the Nazi regime. Once more Hitler pointed out that his actions were always within the legal framework of the time.

This chapter answers the following questions:

• How did the Nazis remove opposition to their regime?
• What was the importance of the Night of the Long Knives?
• What was the police state?
• How was the legal system brought under Nazi control?

Source skills

This chapter reinforces some of the inference and cross-referencing skills from the previous chapters and also gives guidance on the Paper 2 utility question, which is worth eight marks. To get high marks in the utility question you need to examine its content and its Nature, Origin and Purpose (NOP). In this chapter you will focus on the content of a source, and in Chapter 4 you will focus on the Nature, Origin and Purpose of a source (pages 59–61).

How did the Nazis remove opposition to their regime?

Source A The *Reichstag* (parliament) building on fire, 27 February 1933

Task

1. *Work in pairs. Source A shows the* Reichstag *on fire. What do you think the reactions would be if the Houses of Parliament in London burnt down? Explain your answer carefully. (Think about who people might blame and what people might want the government to do.)*

The end of parliamentary democracy

When Hitler became Chancellor, there were only two other Nazis in the Cabinet of twelve – Wilhelm Frick and Hermann Goering. Hitler's position was not strong because the Nazis and his allies, the **Nationalist Party**, did not have a majority in the *Reichstag* and furthermore, President Hindenburg detested him. However, it was soon clear that von Papen's claim that he would be able to control Hitler was utterly wrong.

Hitler immediately called a general election for 5 March hoping it would give him a clear majority in the *Reichstag*. If he controlled parliament then he would be able to make those laws that would be needed to tighten his grip on the nation. It would all be done by the rule of law – Nazi law. Violence and terror were again seen in this election campaign and there were about 70 deaths in the weeks leading up to voting day. Hitler received large amounts of money from leading industrialists to assist his campaign and with access to the media, he knew that Goebbels would be able to put the Nazi message over unceasingly.

One week before the election on 27 February, the *Reichstag* building was set on fire. It is not known who started the fire, but the Nazis arrested Marinus van der Lubbe, a Dutch Communist. This was a wonderful opportunity for Hitler and Goebbels to exploit. They claimed that the Communists were about to stage a takeover.

Source B From the memoirs of Rudolf Diels, Head of the Prussian Police in 1933. He was writing about Hitler's reaction to the *Reichstag* Fire. Diels was writing in 1950

Hitler was standing on a balcony gazing at the red ocean of fire. He swung round towards us... his face had turned quite scarlet with the excitement... Suddenly he started screaming at the top of his voice:

'Now we'll show them! Anyone who stands in our way will be mown down. The German people have been too soft for too long. Every Communist official must be shot. All friends of the Communists must be locked up. And that goes for the Social Democrats too.'

Tasks

2. *How useful is Source B as evidence of the Nazis' attitude to the* Reichstag *Fire?*

3. *What does the artist mean by the caption in Source C? Devise another caption for the photomontage to show who set fire to the Reichstag.*

4. *Find out more about the background and trial of Marinus van der Lubbe.*

5. *Is Source C useful in showing us what happened at the* Reichstag?

6. *How useful is Source D as evidence of events after the* Reichstag *Fire?*

(Tasks 2, 5, 6 are utility questions. You could answer them by looking at the content of the sources only or by looking at content and Nature, Origin and Purpose (NOP). For guidance on content see page 51 in this chapter; for guidance on NOP see Chapter 4, pages 59–61.)

Source C 'Goering – The executioner of the Third Reich'. This is a photomontage by the Communist artist, John Heartfield. A photomontage is made up of several different photographs

Source D Berlin police burn red flags after raiding the homes of Communists, 26 March 1933

The Enabling Bill

Hitler persuaded Hindenburg to sign the 'Decree for the Protection of People and State' on 28 February. This suspended basic **civil rights** and allowed the Nazis to imprison large numbers of their political opponents. Communist and Socialist newspapers were banned. At the election, the Nazis won 288 seats and with the 52 seats of the National Party now had a majority in the *Reichstag*. Despite having a majority Hitler was disappointed because he needed two-thirds of the seats in order to be able to change the constitution.

His next step was to pass the **Enabling Bill**. This would give him and his government full powers for the next four years and would mean that the *Reichstag* would become a rubber stamp for Nazi activities. The Bill was passed but by devious means.

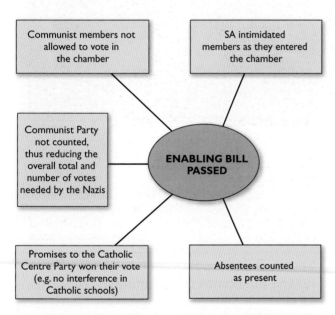

The Enabling Law was passed on 24 March and signalled the end of the Weimar constitution and democracy. Hitler could now move to secure closer control of the nation by means of this new law.

On 14 July 1933, the Law against the Formation of Parties was passed which made the Nazi Party the sole legal political party in Germany. In the November 1933 general election, 95.2 per cent of the electorate voted and the Nazis won 39,638,000 votes. (There was some protest against the Nazis – about 3 million ballot papers were spoilt.)

The removal of rival organisations

With the new Enabling Law, Hitler was now in a position to bring German society into line with Nazi philosophy. This policy was called *Gleichschaltung*. It would create a truly National Socialist state and would mean that every aspect of the social, political and economic life of a German citizen was controlled and monitored by the Nazis.

On 2 May 1933, all trade unions were banned. The Nazis said that a national community had been created and therefore, such organisations were no longer needed. The **Nazi Labour Front** was set up to replace not only trade unions but also employers' groups. Wages were decided by the Labour Front and workers received work-books. These were records of employment and employment depended on ownership of one. Strikes were outlawed and any dissenters would be sent to the new prisons – **concentration camps** – for political re-education. The first concentration camp opened at Dachau in March 1933. There could be no challenge to the Nazi state.

Hitler also broke down the **federal structure** of Germany. There were eighteen *Länder* (districts), and each had its own parliament. On occasions in the Weimar period, some of the *Länder* had caused problems for the President because their political make-up differed and they refused to accept decisions made in the *Reichstag*. President Ebert had issued more than 130 emergency decrees to overrule some of the *Länder*. Hitler decided that the *Länder* were to be run by *Reich* governors and their parliaments were abolished in January 1934. Thus he centralised the country for the first time since its creation in 1871.

Tasks

7. *Work in pairs. You are investigative journalists in Germany 1933. Write an article exposing the links between the* Reichstag *Fire (page 41) and how the Enabling Law was able to be passed.*

8. *What is meant by the term* Gleichschaltung?

9. *Why was* Gleichschaltung *important for the Nazis?*

The army

Hitler was keen to secure the support of the army. By early 1934, there were some in the Nazi Party, such as Röhm, leader of the SA, who wished to incorporate it into the SA. However, Hitler knew that there would be opposition from the generals and this could mean a challenge to his own position. Moreover, if he removed the SA, he could win the support of the army in his bid for the presidency because the army felt threatened by the SA and many of the army leaders did not like its socialist nature. Hindenburg was becoming very frail and Hitler sought to combine his own post and that of President. The support of the army was gained following the Night of the Long Knives (see pages 44–45) when the leaders of the SA were assassinated.

On the death of Hindenburg in August 1934, the army swore allegiance to Hitler who, having combined the posts of Chancellor and President, was now their *Führer*.

> **Source F The army's oath of allegiance to Hitler, August 1934**
>
> *I swear before God to give my unconditional obedience to Adolf Hitler,* Führer *of the* Reich *and of the German people, and I pledge my word as a brave soldier to observe this oath always, even at the peril of my life.*

Tasks

10. *Look at Source E. Can you suggest reasons to explain why photographs such as this were displayed all over Germany?*

11. *How useful is Source F in helping you understand why Hitler felt more secure after the army oath had been made? (Look at the content and Nature, Origin and Purpose of the source. For guidance on content, see page 51 and for NOP see Chapter 4 pages 59–61.)*

What was the importance of the Night of the Long Knives?

The Night of the Long Knives (also known as 'Operation Hummingbird' or 'the Blood Purge') was the purging of Hitler's political and military rivals in the *Sturmabteilung*. You have already seen that one cause of the removal of leaders of the SA was the need to win the support of the army (see page 43). However, in the first months of his chancellorship, Hitler saw the SA as quite a major threat.

The SA had been a key part in the growth of the Nazis and by 1933 they were well known across Germany. Most of the SA were working-class who favoured the socialist views of the Nazi programme. They were hoping that Hitler would introduce reforms to help the workers.

Moreover, Röhm, leader of the SA, wanted to incorporate the army into the SA and was disappointed with Hitler's close relations with industrialists and the army leaders. Röhm wanted more government interference in the running of the country in order to help the ordinary citizens. He wanted to move away from Germany's class structure and bring greater equality. In effect he wanted a social revolution. There was further tension for Hitler because his personal bodyguard, the SS (*Schutzstaffel*), led by Heinrich Himmler, wished to break away from the SA. Goering (Head of the **Gestapo**) wanted to lead the armed forces and hence saw an opponent in Röhm.

Task

1. *What can you learn from Source A about the SA? (Remember how to answer this type of question? For further guidance see page 20.)*

Source A Photograph of Hitler and Röhm with SA troops

Sturmabteilung (SA)	c.3,000,000
Schutzstaffel (SS)	c.52,000
Army	c.100,000

Membership of uniformed services in early 1934

Source B From *Hitler speaks* by H. Rauschning, 1940. Rauschning was a Nazi official who left Germany in 1934 to live in the USA. Here he is describing a conversation with Röhm in 1934. Röhm was drunk when he said the following

Adolf's a swine. . . He only associates with those on the right. . . His old friends aren't good enough for him. Adolf is turning into a gentleman. What he wants is to sit on the hill top and pretend he is God. He knows exactly what I want. . . The generals are a lot of old fogeys. . . I'm the nucleus of the new army.

Tasks

2. Look back at the 25 Point Programme in Chapter 1, page 16 and the text about Röhm's ideas about a social revolution on page 44.

   a) Discuss in class which parts of the programme match Röhm's views.

   b) Explain why Hitler and some of his industrialist supporters were concerned about Röhm.

3. Look at Source B and the text about Röhm and the SA. How useful is Source B in helping you understand why Röhm was unhappy with Hitler? (Look at the content and Nature, Origin and Purpose of the source. For guidance on content, see page 51 and for NOP see Chapter 4 pages 59–61.)

Hitler took action in June, following information from Himmler that Röhm was about to seize power. On 30 June 1934 Röhm and the main leaders of the SA were shot by members of the SS. Hitler also took the opportunity to settle some old scores: von Schleicher was murdered, as was Gregor Strasser, a key figure among those Nazis with socialist views similar to Röhm. About 400 people were murdered in the **purge**.

Source C From a report of the *Reich* cabinet meeting about the Night of the Long Knives, printed in the *Völkischer Beobachter* (official Nazi newspaper), 5 July 1934

Defence Minister General von Blomberg thanked the Führer in the name of the Reich Cabinet and the army for his determined and courageous action, by which he saved the German people from a civil war. The Führer had shown greatness as a statesman and a soldier. This had aroused in the hearts of. . . the German people a vow of service, devotion and loyalty in this grave hour.

Source D From Hitler's speech to the *Reichstag* on 13 July 1934, justifying his actions concerning the SA

In the circumstances I had to make but one decision. If disaster was to be prevented at all, action had to be taken with lightning speed. Only a ruthless and bloody intervention might still perhaps stifle the spread of revolt. If anyone reproaches me and asks why I did not resort to the regular courts of justice for conviction of the offenders, then all I can say is, 'In this hour I was responsible for the fate of the German people and therefore I became the supreme judge of the German people'.

Task

4. Study Sources B, C and D. Does Source D support the evidence of Sources B and C about the threat of the SA? Explain your answer. (Remember how to answer this type of question? For further guidance see pages 36–37.)

The impact of the Night of the Long Knives

The Night of the Long Knives is often seen as the turning point for Hitler's rule in Germany. He eradicated would-be opponents and secured the support of the army. The SA was relegated to a minor role and if there was any doubt about Hitler's rule, it was now clear that fear and terror would play significant roles.

Source E A cartoon from the *London Evening Standard*, 3 July 1934. The caption reads: 'They salute with both hands now'. Goering is standing to Hitler's right dressed as a Viking hero and Goebbels is on his knees behind Hitler. The words 'Unkept promises' appear on the paper in front of the SA and 'the double cross' above and below Hitler's armband

THEY SALUTE WITH BOTH HANDS NOW.

Source F A cartoon published in the *Daily Express*, 3 July 1934. The caption is 'Will members of the audience kindly keep their seats'. Members of the audience include representatives from the USA, UK and the USSR

Tasks

5. *How useful are Sources E and F as evidence of the Night of the Long Knives? Explain your answer. Look very carefully at the content here, especially the words 'broken promises' and 'double cross'. (This is a utility question. For further guidance see pages 51 and 59–61.)*

6. *What were the results of the Night of the Long Knives? Construct a circle with the 'Night of the Long Knives' at the centre. Look at the points below and consider the results of the purge for each, working out who gained most from the Night of the Long Knives, and who gained least, or lost. Then place them around the circle starting with the one who benefited most at the top and work in a clockwise direction:*

- *the army*
- *the SA*
- *Hitler's rivals*
- *the SS*
- *Hitler's own position*
- *Himmler*
- *Goering.*

What was the police state?

Source A An auxiliary policeman (SA drafted into the police) guarding arrested Communists in 1933

Task

1. *What can you learn from Source A about Nazi police methods? (Remember how to answer this type of question? For further guidance see page 20.)*

You have read earlier how the Nazis wanted to control all aspects of German life and used the policy of *Gleichschaltung* (see page 42) in order to achieve this. If **indoctrination** did not work, then force and terror were used. The Nazis used their own organisations to instil fear into the people. The SS, **SD** (*Sicherheitsdienst*, Security Service) and Gestapo were the main ones and in 1936 they were all brought under the control of Himmler.

Biography Heinrich Himmler 1900–45

1900 Born near Munich
1918 Joined the army
1923 Joined the Nazi Party and participated in the Munich *Putsch*
1929 Appointed leader of the SS
1930 Elected as a member of parliament
1934 Organised the Night of the Long Knives
1936 Head of all police agencies in Germany
1945 Committed suicide

The role of the SS (*Schutzstaffel*)

Source B From a speech by Himmler to the Committee for Police Law at the Academy of German Law, 1936

Right from the start, I have taken the view that it does not matter in the least if our actions are against some clause in the law; in my work for my Führer and the nation, I do what my conscience and common sense tell me is right. . . .

Task

2. *What can you learn from Source B about Himmler's view of the law? (Remember how to answer this type of question? For further guidance see page 20.)*

The SS had been formed in 1925 to act as a bodyguard unit for Hitler and was led by Heinrich Himmler after 1929. Himmler built up the SS until it had established a clear visible identity – members wore black. They showed total obedience to the *Führer*. By 1934 the SS had more than 50,000 members who were to be fine examples of the **Aryan** race and were expected to marry racially pure wives.

After the Night of the Long Knives, the SS became responsible for the removal of all opposition within Germany. Within the SS the Security Service (SD) had the task of maintaining security within the party and then the country.

Source C An extract from a book on Nazism, written in 1974

Hitler needed an organisation which would not feel restrained by the law. It would act with utter ruthlessness and would be dedicated to expressing his will and the ideas of the Nazi movement. He found what he needed in the SS.

The Gestapo

The Gestapo (*Geheimestaatspolizei* – secret state police) was set up in 1933 by Goering and in 1936 it came under the control of Himmler and the SS. By 1939, the Gestapo was the most important police section of the Nazi state. It could arrest and imprison those suspected of opposing the state. The most likely destination would be a concentration camp run by the SS. It has been estimated that, by 1939, there were about 160,000 people under arrest for political crimes.

Source D An incident reported in the Rhineland, July 1938

In a café, a 64-year-old woman remarked to her companion at the table: 'Mussolini [leader of Italy] has more political sense in one of his boots than Hitler has in his brain.' The remark was overheard and five minutes later the woman was arrested by the Gestapo who had been alerted by telephone.

Task

3. *Study Sources B, C and D. Does Source D support the evidence of Sources B and C about the law in Nazi Germany? (Remember how to answer this type of question? For further guidance see pages 36–37.)*

How was the legal system brought under Nazi control?

Source A Judge Roland Freisler, State Secretary at the *Reich* Ministry of Justice. Here, he is presiding over a People's Court

Source B From *Hitler's Table Talk*. After 1941, all Hitler's private conversations at his military headquarters were recorded by Martin Bormann, Hitler's secretary. This one is from 1942

Justice is no aim in itself. We must exterminate the idea that it is the judge's function to let the law prevail even if the old should perish. This is pure madness. The main task is to secure the social order.

Even though the Nazis controlled the *Reichstag* and could make laws, Hitler wanted to ensure that all laws were interpreted in a Nazi fashion. The law courts therefore had to experience *Gleichschaltung*, just as any other part of society. Some judges were removed and all had to become members of the National Socialist League for the Maintenance of Law. This meant that Nazi views were upheld in the courts. In October 1933, the German Lawyers Front was established and there were more than 10,000 members by the end of the year.

Task

1. *What do you think Hitler meant in Source B when he said 'The main task is to secure the social order'?*

In 1934, a new People's Court was established to try cases of treason. The judges were loyal Nazis. Judges knew that the Minister of Justice would check to see if they had been lenient and sometimes Hitler would alter sentences if he felt that they were too soft.

By the end of 1934, Hitler controlled the *Reichstag*, the army and the legal system. The Nazi police and security organisations had wormed their way into the fabric of society and it was now almost impossible for anyone to escape the power and grip of the Nazis.

Source C An explanation of the judge's role, put forward by Nazi legal expert, Professor Karl Eckhardt in 1936

The judge is to safeguard the order of the racial community, to prosecute all acts harmful to the community and to arbitrate in disagreements. The National Socialist ideology, especially as expressed in the party programme and in the speeches of our Führer, is the basis for interpreting legal sources.

Source D Decree for the Protection of the Nationalist Movement against Malicious Attacks upon the Government, 21 March 1933

Whoever purposely makes or circulates a statement of a factual nature which is grossly exaggerated or which may seriously harm the welfare of the Reich is to be punished with imprisonment of up to two years. . . .

Source E An extract from the law setting out to change the Penal Code, 28 June 1935

*National Socialism considers every attack on the welfare of the national community as wrong. **In future, therefore, wrong may be committed in Germany even in cases where there is no law against what is being done.***

The law-maker cannot give a complete set of rules covering all situations which may occur in life; he therefore entrusts the judge with filling in the remaining gaps.

Tasks

2. What can you learn from Source A (page 49) and Source C about the role of judges in Nazi Germany? (Remember how to answer this type of question? See page 20 for guidance.)

3. How useful are Sources D and E in helping you to understand how the Nazis controlled people in Germany? (Here you need only look at the content of the source. See page 51 for guidance. In the examination you will need to analyse content and the NOP, see pages 59–61.)

4. Look at Source E. Can you suggest reasons why the sentence in bold was so crucial to the Nazis?

Examination practice

The utility (usefulness) question is worth eight marks and will ask you to evaluate two sources. For this question you need to look at the content of the sources and their nature, origin and purpose (NOP). In this chapter we will look at only the content. In Chapter 4, you will look at the NOP and how to bring in source content.

Remember:

- **All** sources are useful.
- When you look at a source, you need to understand the context of the source, i.e. what is happening around the source. This means that you must know the topic well.
- When you select information from the content of the source, you must be able to add to it from your own knowledge. In effect, you are measuring what you know against what the source says.

Question 1 – utility (content only)

How useful is Source A as evidence of Nazi election tactics?

Remember that here we are only concerned with the **content** of the source.

How to answer

- Look for any words/ideas that are related to the topic.
- For each point draw an arrow from the source and write down the point.
- In a different colour, explain each point further – add your own knowledge to it. When you can see the colours building up, you know that you are taking information from the source and also adding to it.
- You may only find two or three points. Sometimes you may find that something is exaggerated – you will cover this in the next chapter.
- Then you should be in a position to write an explanation of why the source is useful.
- Always begin your answer by saying 'The source is useful because…'.
- Always relate your answer back to the question – here you must write about election tactics.

See next page for examples of notes you could make about Source A.

Source A A Nazi election campaign poster from Saxony, early 1930s. The caption reads 'A Saxony free of **Marxist** rubbish!' At the foot of the poster, it reads 'Vote National Socialist List 7'

Example

Use of swastika: symbol easily recognised. Red star of Communists is small in comparison

Strong German man: typical ideal figure fits in with racial theory

Use of the word Marxist: brings fear – Hitler hated the Marxists – such a poster spread fear, e.g. among middle classes, industrialists

Images of Marxists unflattering: makes them look inferior – part of the process of belittling all non-Germans

Overall: a poster, Nazis used lots of these – simple but has many meanings to it. Hitler and Goebbels kept the messages simple in order to win votes.

Question 2 – utility (content only)

Now have a go yourself.
How useful is Source B as evidence of support for the Nazis in election campaigns?

Source B From the book *I knew Hitler* by K. Lüdecke, written in 1938. Here, he is describing the July 1932 election campaign

As I walked through the Berlin streets, the Nazi Party flags were everywhere. Huge posters, pictures and Nazi slogans screamed from windows with messages about honour, duty, national solidarity and social justice, bread, liberty and the beauty of sacrifice – all proclaiming the superb skill with which Hitler had been influencing the masses.

The Nazi State, 1933–39

Source A Nazi propaganda poster of 1933 which proclaims 'We Remain Comrades'

Tasks

1. *What message is the poster trying to get across?*

2. *How does it get across this message?*

During the course of this chapter you will find out why propaganda was of such importance to the Nazis.

Once Hitler had removed opposition, he had to create a state which believed in and supported Nazi ideals. This was achieved through skilful use of propaganda under Goebbels whose Ministry of Propaganda controlled all aspects of the media, the arts, entertainment and even sport. Of particular importance were the young who were the future of the **Third Reich**. Furthermore, the Nazis were determined that Germans would owe their first allegiance to the *Führer* rather than to either the Catholic or Protestant Churches.

This chapter answers the following questions:

• What propaganda methods were used?
• In what ways did the Nazis control the young?
• How did the Nazis control the arts and sport?
• Why were religious groups persecuted by the Nazis?

Source skills

This chapter gives you guidance on the third source question on Paper 2. This is the utility question which asks you to decide the usefulness of two sources. It is worth eight marks. In Chapter 3 you looked at the utility of the contents of a source. In this chapter you will concentrate on the Nature, Origin and Purpose (NOP).

What propaganda methods were used?

Goebbels used his Ministry of Public Propaganda and Enlightenment to control the thoughts, beliefs and opinions of the German people. It was important for the long-term future of the Third Reich that the majority of the population believed in the ideals of the Nazi Party. All aspects of the media were censored and skilfully manipulated by Goebbels. He used a variety of methods.

Source A Goebbels explaining the use of propaganda

The finest kind of propaganda does not reveal itself. The best propaganda is that which works invisibly, penetrating every cell of life in such a way that the public has no idea of the aims of the propagandist.

Newspapers

Non-Nazi newspapers and magazines were closed down. Editors were told what they could print.

Source B Orders from the Ministry of Propaganda, 1935

Photos showing members of the Reich government at dining tables in front of rows of bottles must not be published in the future. This has given the absurd impression that members of the government are living it up.

Rallies

An annual mass rally was held at Nuremberg to advertise the power of the Nazi state and spectacular parades were held on other special occasions. Local rallies and marches were led by the SA and the **Hitler Youth** *(see page 57).*

Radio

All radio stations were placed under Nazi control. Cheap mass-produced radios were sold. Sets were installed in cafes and factories and loudspeakers were placed in streets. It was important that the Nazi message was heard.

Source C A photograph showing workers listening to a broadcast by Hitler

Cinema

Goebbels also realised the popularity of the cinema, with over 100 films made each year and audiences topping 250 million in 1933. He was one of the first to realise its potential for propaganda. All film plots were shown to Goebbels before going into production. He realised that many Germans were bored by overtly political films. Instead love stories and thrillers were given pro-Nazi slants. One of the best known was Hitlerjunge Quex (1933) which tells the story of a boy who broke away from a Communist family to join the Hitler Youth, only to be murdered by Communists. All film performances were accompanied by a 45-minute official newsreel which glorified Hitler and Germany and publicised Nazi achievements.*

Posters

Posters were cleverly used to put across the Nazi message with the young particularly targeted.

A propaganda poster of 1934 which says 'Loyalty, Honour and Order'

Books

All books were carefully censored and controlled to put across the Nazi message. Encouraged by Goebbels, students in Berlin burnt 20,000 books written by Jews, Communists, and anti-Nazi university professors in a massive bonfire in May 1933. Many writers were persuaded or forced to write books which praised Hitler's achievements.

Students and stormtroopers burning books in Berlin in May 1933

Source D From a report on public opinion in Germany, written in 1936

A large section of the population no longer reads a newspaper. Basically, the population has no interest in the newspapers. The Nazis try to turn everyone into committed National Socialists. They will never succeed in that. People tend to turn away from Nazi propaganda. One cannot speak of popular enthusiasm for Nazism.

Jokes!

'A Law Against Malicious Gossip' in 1934 forbade the telling of anti-Nazi jokes and stories. The penalties for being caught doing so were fines or prison.

Tasks

1. *What can you learn from Source A about Goebbels' use of propaganda? (Remember how to answer this type of question? For further guidance see page 20.)*

2. *Does Source C support the evidence of Source D about the effect of Nazi propaganda? Explain your answer. (Remember how to answer this type of question? For further guidance see page 36.)*

3. *The following newspaper article has been given to the Ministry of Propaganda for censorship.*

Yesterday our tired looking Führer, *wearing his spectacles, met members of the Hitler Youth. However only a small number turned up and our leader only had time to talk to one or two. He later attended a party to celebrate the anniversary of him becoming Chancellor. Lots of wine was consumed.*

a) *What will they remove or change?*

b) *Rewrite the article for publication.*

In what ways did the Nazis control the young?

Hitler saw the young as the future of the Third Reich. They had to be converted to Nazi ideals. This was achieved through control of education and the Hitler Youth.

Education

Everyone in Germany had to go to school until the age of fourteen. After that schooling was optional. Boys and girls went to separate schools.

Teachers

They had to swear an oath of loyalty to Hitler and join the **Nazi Teachers' League**. Teachers had to promote Nazi ideals in the classroom.

Curriculum

This was changed to prepare students for their future roles. Hitler wanted healthy, fit men and women so 15 per cent of time was devoted to physical education. With the boys the emphasis was on preparation for the military. Girls took needlework and home crafts, especially cookery, to become good homemakers and mothers. New subjects such as race studies (see page 68) were introduced to put across Nazi ideas on race and population control. Children were taught how to measure their skulls and to classify racial types. Also they were taught that Aryans were superior and should not marry inferior races such as Jews.

Textbooks

These were rewritten to fit the Nazi view of history and racial purity. *Mein Kampf* became a standard text.

Lessons

These began and ended with the students saluting and saying '*Heil Hitler*'. Nazi themes were presented through every subject. Maths problems dealt with social issues. Geography lessons were used to show how Germany was surrounded by hostile neighbours. In history lessons, students were taught about the evils of Communism and the Treaty of Versailles.

Source A A question from a maths textbook, 1933

The Jews are aliens in Germany. In 1933 there were 66,060,000 inhabitants of the German Reich of whom 499,862 were Jews. What is the percentage of aliens in Germany?

Tasks

1. *What can you learn from Source A about the aims of Nazi education? (Remember how to answer this type of question? For further guidance see page 20.)*

2. *Choose a subject. See if you can devise a question or problem which would reflect Nazi ideals, for example, hatred of Communism, the desire to destroy the Treaty of Versailles, or to make Germany great.*

The Hitler Youth

The Nazis also wanted to control the young in their spare time. This was achieved through the Hitler Youth.

- All other youth organisations were banned.
- From 1936 membership was compulsory.
- By 1939 there were seven million members.

Hitler Youth males	Hitler Youth females
Source B A recruiting poster for the Hitler Youth, 1933	**Source C** A recruiting poster for the Young Girls which says 'Every ten-year-old to us'

Boys joined the German Young People at the age of ten. From fourteen to eighteen they became members of the Hitler Youth. They learned Nazi songs and ideas and took part in athletics, hiking and camping. As they got older they practised marching, map reading and military skills. Many enjoyed the comradeship. It's also possible they enjoyed the fact that their camps were often near to those of the League of German Maidens.	Girls joined the Young Girls at the age of ten. From fourteen to eighteen they joined the League of German Maidens. They did much the same as the boys except they also learned domestic skills in preparation for motherhood and marriage and there was much less emphasis on military training.

Source D The memories of a Hitler Youth leader

What I liked about the Hitler Youth was the comradeship. I was full of enthusiasm when I joined the Young People at the age of ten. I can still remember how deeply moved I was when I heard the club mottoes: 'Young People are hard. They can keep a secret. They are loyal. They are comrades.' And then there were the trips! Is anything nicer than enjoying the splendours of the homeland in the company of one's comrades?

Tasks

3. *What can you learn from Source D about the Hitler Youth? (Remember how to answer this type of question? For further guidance see page 20.)*

4. *You have been asked by your local Hitler Youth to produce a poster promoting the organisation. You could use either Source B or C as the illustration for your poster and get more ideas from Source D.*

Teenage rebels

Not all young people accepted the Nazi ideas. Indeed by the 1930s gangs began to appear on street corners. They played their own music and boys and girls were free to be together. Many grew their hair long and wore their own choice of clothes. Some went hunting for members of the Hitler Youth and beat them up.

One such group was the Edelweiss Pirates. They listened to forbidden Swing music and daubed walls with anti-Nazi graffiti. They could be recognised by their badges, for example the edelweiss or skull and crossbones. They wore check shirts, dark short trousers and white socks. The earliest recorded groups were in 1934 and by 1939 they had a membership of 2,000.

Source E A photograph of members of the Edelweiss Pirates

Source F Verse from an Edelweiss Pirates' Song

Hitler's power may lay us low,
And keep us locked in chains,
But we will smash the chains one day.
We'll be free again.
We've got fists and we can fight.
We've got knives and we'll get them out.

Task

5. *Using Sources E, F and G explain why you think some teenagers rebelled against the Hitler Youth.*

Source G From a British magazine, 1938

There seems little enthusiasm for the Hitler Youth, with membership falling. Many no longer want to be commanded, but wish to do as they like. Usually only a third of a group appears for roll-call. At evening meetings it is a great event if 20 turn up out of 80, but usually there are only about 10 or 12.

Examination practice

Chapter 3 (page 51) explained how to evaluate the utility of the contents of the source. In this chapter we will concentrate on NOP – the nature, origin and purpose of each source. You must analyse these aspects to reach top marks (7/8 marks).

In order to reach higher level marks for this question you have to explain the value (usefulness) and limitations of the NOP of each source. This is found in the provenance of the source – the information given above or below it. A good tip is to highlight or underline key words in the

provenance which show either the utility or limitations of the source. An example of how you could approach this is given in Source A below. On page 60 is a reminder of what to consider for the NOP.

Question 1 – utility

How useful is Source A as evidence of activities of the Hitler Youth in the 1930s?

How to answer

Utility

Limitations

Nature. This suggests it is useful because the letter would not have been censored and the Hitler Youth Member would be giving his genuine thoughts on life in the camp.

Nature. This is of limited use because there is no indication to whom the letter was written.

Origin. This is useful because it was written by someone who actually experienced the Hitler Youth in the mid-1930s. It is an eyewitness account.

Source A Hitler Youth member, private letter, 1936

How did we live in Camp S—, which is supposed to be an example to all the camps? We practically didn't have a minute of the day to ourselves. This isn't camp life, no sir! It's military barrack life! Drill starts right after a meagre breakfast. We would like to have athletics but there isn't any. Instead we have military exercises, down in the mud, till the tongue hangs out of your mouth. And we have only one wish: sleep, sleep. . . .

Origin. It only gives the view of one Hitler Youth member which may not be typical. Indeed many members seemed to enjoy the camps.

Purpose. This is useful because it is not the usual propaganda about the Hitler Youth but someone who is trying to persuade the reader that the movement was not an enjoyable experience.

Purpose. This also has limitations. The writer may have exaggerated the downside of life in the camp in order to convince the reader that the Hitler Youth was not an enjoyable experience.

Here is a reminder of what else to consider for the NOP.

N Nature of the source.
What type of source is it? A speech, a photograph, a cartoon, a letter, an extract from a diary? How will the nature of the source affect its utility? For example, a private letter is often very useful because the person who wrote it generally gives their honest views.

O Origin of the source.
Who wrote or produced the source? Are their views worth knowing? Are they giving a one-sided view? When was it produced? It could be an eyewitness account. What are the advantages and disadvantages of eyewitness accounts?

P Purpose of the source.
For what reason was the source produced? For example, the purpose of adverts is to make you buy the products. People usually make speeches to get your support. How will this affect the utility of the source?

Question 2 – utility

How useful is Source B as evidence of the activities of the League of German Maidens?

Source B A photograph taken in 1936 of members of the League of German Maidens going on a hike

Now have a go yourself

Include the value and limitations of the contents of the source. If you need further guidance on this look back to page 51 (Chapter 3).

Make a copy of the grid opposite and use it to plan your answer.

	Value	Limitations
Nature		
Origin		
Purpose		
Contents		

Question 3 – utility

How useful are Sources C and D as evidence of education in Nazi Germany? (8 marks)

How to answer

In the examination you will be asked to explain the utility of two sources.

- Explain the value and limitations of the content of each source.
- Explain the value and limitations of the NOP of each source.
- In your conclusion, give a final judgement on the relative value of each source. For example, one source might provide one view of an event; the other source a different view.

Make a copy of the following grid and use it to plan your answer.

Source C A teacher with her pupils during a history lesson, *c.* 1933

Source D From the memoirs, written in the 1960s, of a German who was a student in the 1930s

No one in our class ever read Mein Kampf. *I myself only used the book for quotations. In general we didn't do much about Nazi ideas. Anti-Semitism wasn't mentioned much by our teachers except through Richard Wagner's essay 'The Jews in Music'. We did, however, do a lot of physical education and cookery.*

Source C	Value	Limitations
Contents		
Nature		
Origin		
Purpose		
Source D		
Contents		
Nature		
Origin		
Purpose		

Here is a writing frame to help you:

Source C is useful because (contents) ....
....

Moreover Source C is also useful because (NOP) ....

Source C has limitations including (contents) ..
....

Source C is also of limited use because (NOP) ..
....

Source D is useful because (contents) ....
....

Moreover Source D is also useful because (NOP)...

Source D has limitations including (contents) ..
....

Source D is also of limited use because (NOP) .
....

In conclusion Sources C and D are useful because they...................................

How did the Nazis control the arts and sport?

The arts and sport were also used by the Nazis as methods of propaganda. Goebbels set up the Reich Chamber of Culture. Musicians, writers and actors had to be members of the Chamber. Any that were thought to be unsuitable were banned. Many left Germany in protest at these conditions.

Music
Hitler hated modern music. Jazz, which was 'black' music, was seen as racially inferior and banned. Instead the Nazis encouraged traditional German folk music together with the classical music of Bach and Beethoven.

Theatre
Theatre was to concentrate on German history and political drama. Cheap theatre tickets were available to encourage people to see plays often with a Nazi political or racial theme.

Architecture
Hitler took a particular interest in architecture. He encouraged the 'monumental style' for public buildings. These were large buildings made of stone which were often copies from ancient Greece or Rome and showed the power of the Third Reich. In addition the 'country style' was used for family homes and hostels – traditional buildings with shutters to encourage pride in Germany's past.

Art
Hitler had earned a living as an artist and believed he was an expert in this area. He hated modern art (any art developed under the Weimar Republic), which he believed was backward, unpatriotic and Jewish. This was banned. In its place, he encouraged art which highlighted Germany's past greatness and the strength and power of the Third Reich. He wanted art to reject the weak and ugly, and to glorify healthy, strong heroes.

Paintings showed:

- the Nazi idea of the simple peasant life
- hard work as heroic
- the perfect Aryan. Young German men and women were shown to have perfect bodies
- women in their preferred role as housewives and mothers.

Source A *The Family*. This was painted in 1938 by a Nazi artist, Walter Willrich

Sport
Sport was encouraged at school and in the Hitler Youth. Hitler wanted a healthy and fit nation – the boys were to be the soldiers of the future and the girls were to produce as many children as possible. Success in sport was also important to promote the Nazi regime.

The major sporting showcase was the 1936 Olympics which was staged in Berlin. Everything about the games was designed to impress the outside world. With the media of 49 countries there in strength, the Nazis could show the world that Germany was a modern, well-organised society and that Aryans were superior. For the most part the Olympics was a great public relations success.

However, there was an exception, as the case study below shows.

The Olympic stadium was the largest in the world and could hold 110,000 spectators

Signs declaring 'Jews not wanted' were removed. Foreign visitors got a positive image of Germany.

Every detail was carefully stage-managed and news reports were controlled

Germany won more medals than any other nation – 33 gold, 26 silver and 30 bronze

All filming was under the direction of Leni Riefenstahl. All camera crews had to be approved by her and all shots supervised

Case study Jesse Owens

The Berlin Olympics was meant to highlight the superiority of the Aryan race through the success of the German athletes. Hitler's plans were sabotaged by the success of the black athletes in the US Olympic team, especially Jesse Owens. Owens won the 100 metres, 200 metres, long jump and the 4 x 100 metres relay. He broke Olympic records eleven times and was very popular with the German crowd. There were nine other black US athletes in the track and field events. Between them, they won seven gold medals. Hitler was not amused! He refused to present medals to the black athletes.

Source B The *Reich* Youth Leader, Baldur von Schirach, explains what Hitler said to him after Owens' 100 metres victory

'The Americans should be ashamed of themselves, letting Negroes win their medals for them. I shall not shake hands with this Negro. Do you really think that I will allow myself to be shaking hands with a Negro?'

Tasks

1. *How useful is Source A as evidence of the Nazi use of art in the Third Reich? (Remember how to answer this type of question? For further guidance see pages 51 and 59.)*

2. *What can you learn from Source B about Hitler's attitude to Owens? (Remember how to answer this type of question? For further guidance see page 20.)*

3. *Imagine mobile phones existed in 1936. You witness Owens' victories and Hitler's reactions. Put together a text of the events to send to a friend. You may use text language. Maximum 160 letters.*

Why were religious groups persecuted by the Nazis?

Nazi ideals were opposed to the beliefs and values of the Christian Church.

Nazism	Christianity
Glorified strength and violence	Teaches love and forgiveness
Despised the weak	Helps the weak
Believed in racial superiority	Respect for all people
Saw Hitler as god-like figure	Belief in God

However, Hitler could not immediately persecute Christianity as Germany was essentially a Christian country. Almost two-thirds of the population was Protestant, most of whom lived in the north; almost one-third was Catholic, most of whom lived in the south.

The Catholic Church

In 1933 Hitler saw the Catholic Church as a threat to his Nazi state:

- Catholics owed their first allegiance not to Hitler but to the Pope. They had divided loyalties.
- There were Catholic schools and youth organisations whose message to the young was at odds with that of the Nazi Party.
- The Catholics consistently supported the Centre Party. Hitler intended to remove this party.

At first, however, Hitler decided to co-operate with the Catholic Church. In July 1933 he signed a **concordat** or agreement with the Pope. The Pope agreed that the Catholic Church would stay out of politics if Hitler agreed not to interfere with the Church. Within a few months Hitler had broken this agreement.

- Priests were harassed and arrested. Many criticised the Nazis and ended up in concentration camps.
- Catholic schools were interfered with and eventually abolished.
- Catholic youth movements closed down.
- Monasteries were closed.

In 1937 Pope Pius XI made his famous statement 'With Burning Anxiety' in which he attacked the Nazi system.

Source A From police reports in Bavaria in 1937 and 1938

The influence of the Catholic Church on the population is so strong that the Nazi spirit cannot penetrate. The local population is ever under the strong influence of the priests. These people prefer to believe what the priests say from the pulpit than the words of the best Nazi speakers.

The Protestant Church

There were some Protestants who admired Hitler. They were called 'German Christians'. Their leader was Ludwig Müller who became the *Reich* bishop, which means national leader, in September 1933.

Source B A Protestant pastor speaking in a 'German Christian' church in 1937

We all know that if the Third Reich were to collapse today, Communism would come in its place. Therefore we must show loyalty to the Führer who has saved us from Communism and given us a better future. Support the 'German Christian' Church.

Source C A photograph of *Reich* bishop Müller after the consecration of the Gustav-Adolf church, Berlin, 1933

However, many Protestants opposed Nazism, which they believed conflicted greatly with their own Christian beliefs. They were led by Pastor Martin Niemöller, a First World War submarine commander. In December 1933 they set up the Pastors' Emergency League for those who opposed Hitler. In the following year they set up their own Confessional Church. Niemöller was arrested in 1937 and sent to a concentration camp. The Confessional Church was banned.

Source D From a history of Nazi Germany, 1997

The Nazis never destroyed the established Churches in Germany. They made it difficult for Christians to worship but the churches remained open and services were held. However, Hitler succeeded in his aim of weakening the Churches as a source of resistance to his policies.

Tasks

1. Eventually Hitler would have completely removed the Christian Churches and replaced them with a Nazi Church. Who or what would have taken the place of the following:

- God
- the Bible
- the cross as a symbol
- the disciples?

2. How useful are Sources A and C as evidence of the reactions of German Christians to the Nazis? (Remember how to answer this type of question? For further guidance see pages 51 and 59.)

3. 'Hitler was successful in destroying support for the Christian Churches in Germany, 1933–39.' Use Sources A, B, C and D, and your own knowledge, to explain whether you agree with this view. (This is a synthesis question. For further guidance see page 76.)

Examination practice

Question 1 – utility

How useful are Sources A and B as evidence of propaganda in Nazi Germany? (8 marks)

Source A An official photograph of Hitler speaking at the 1938 Nuremberg Rally

Source B Orders from the Propaganda Ministry, March 1934, which were advertised in national newspapers

Attention! The Führer is speaking on the radio. On Wednesday 21 March, the Führer is speaking on all German stations from 11 a.m. to 11.50 a.m. The district party headquarters have ordered that all factory owners, department stores, offices, shops, pubs and blocks of flats put up loudspeakers an hour before the broadcast of the Führer's speech so that the whole workforce can participate fully in the broadcast.

Make a copy of the grid and use it to plan your answer.

Source A	Value	Limitations
Contents		
Nature		
Origin		
Purpose		
Source B		
Contents		
Nature		
Origin		
Purpose		

Racism and the treatment of minorities

Source A From the daughter of the US Ambassador in Germany, 1939

As we were coming out of the hotel we saw a crowd gathering in the middle of the street. We stopped to find out what it was all about. There was a tram in the centre of the road from which a young girl was being brutally pushed and shoved. She looked ghastly. Her head had been shaved clean of hair and she was wearing a placard which said 'I have offered myself to a Jew'.

Source B From a private letter by a Jewish refugee, 1933

On the blackest day of all Saturdays big trucks patrolled the Berlin streets from which Nazis shouted down through loudspeakers: 'Down with the Jews!'; 'Jews, die like beasts!' One of the most popular songs of these inhumane beasts was: 'If Jewish blood flows from the knife, things will go much better.' The words for this song were written by a Nazi poet.

Tasks

1. What does Source A suggest about attitudes to the Jews in Nazi Germany?

2. Does Source B support the evidence of Source A about attitudes to Jews in Nazi Germany? Explain your answer.

These two sources provide evidence of the **anti-Semitism** which was typical of Nazi Germany. In order to win support in the years before 1932 Hitler had used the Jews as the scapegoats for many of Germany's problems including defeat in the First World War and the Treaty of Versailles. Once in power, the Nazi propaganda machine was used to turn more and more Germans against the Jews and justify a policy of persecution.

This chapter answers the following questions:

- What was the Nazi theory of the racial state?
- Why did the Nazis persecute the Jews?
- How did the lives of German Jews change in the years 1933–39?
- Which other groups were persecuted?
- What opposition was there to Nazi rule?

Source skills

This chapter gives you guidance on the fourth source question on Paper 2 – the synthesis question. This question asks you to use the sources and your own knowledge to discuss an interpretation. The question is worth twelve marks.

What was the Nazi theory of the racial state?

Central to Nazi policy was the creation of a pure German state. This meant treating all non-German groups, especially the Jews, as second-class citizens. Hitler's theory of race was based on the idea of the 'master race' and the 'subhumans'. He tried to back up this theory by saying that the Bible showed there were only two races – the Jews and the Aryans – and that God had a special purpose for the Aryans.

Master race

The Nazis believed that the Germans were a pure race of Aryan descent – from the *Herrenvolk* or Master Race. They were shown in art as blond, blue-eyed, tall, lean and athletic – a people fit to master the world. However, this race had been contaminated by the 'subhumans'.

Subhumans

Jews and **Slavs** on the other hand were the *Untermenschen* or subhumans. Nazi propaganda portrayed Jews as evil moneylenders. Hitler regarded the Jews as an evil force and was convinced of their involvement in a world conspiracy to destroy civilisation.

Making the master race

Hitler believed that Germany's future was dependent on the creation of a pure Aryan racial state. This would be achieved by:

- selective breeding
- destroying the Jews.

Source B A poster from an exhibition, used by the Nazis to turn people against the Jews, with the caption 'The Eternal Jew'

GROSSE POLITISCHE SCHAU IM BIBLIOTHEKSBAU DES DEUTSCHEN MUSEUMS ZU MÜNCHEN · AB 8. NOVEMBER 1937 · TÄGLICH GEÖFFNET VON 10-21 UHR

Selective breeding meant preventing anyone who did not conform to the Aryan type from having children. The SS were part of the drive for selective breeding. They recruited men who were of Aryan blood, tall, fair-haired and blue-eyed. They were only allowed to marry women of Aryan blood.

Tasks

1. *What can you learn from Source A about Hitler's attitude to the Jews? (Remember how to answer this type of question? For further guidance see page 20.)*

2. *What message does Source B give about Jews?*

Why did the Nazis persecute the Jews?

Hitler and the Nazi Party were by no means the first to think of the Jews as different and treat them with hostility as outsiders. Anti-Semitism goes back to the Middle Ages.

Source A From *Mein Kampf*

Was there any form of filth or crime without at least one Jew involved in it? If you cut continuously into such a sore, you find, like a maggot in a rotting body, often dazzled by the light – a Jew.

Why were the Jews persecuted?

Jewish people have been persecuted throughout history, for example in England during the Middle Ages. This is because Jewish people stood out as different in regions across Europe. They had a different religion and different customs. Some Christians blamed the Jews for the execution of Christ and argued that Jews should be punished forever. Some Jews became moneylenders and became quite wealthy. This increased resentment and suspicion from people who owed them money or were jealous of their success.

Hitler had spent several years in Vienna where there was a long tradition of anti-Semitism. He lived as a down-and-out and resented the wealth of many of the Viennese Jews. In the 1920s he used the Jews as scapegoats for all society's problems. He blamed them for Germany's defeat in the First World War, hyperinflation in 1923 and the Depression of 1929.

Hitler was determined to create a pure racial state. This did not include the 100,000 Jews who were living in Germany. He wanted to eliminate the Jews from German society. He had no master-plan for achieving this, however, and until the beginning of the Second World War, a great deal of Nazi Jewish policy was unco-ordinated.

Source B A Nazi cartoon with the title 'Jewish department store octopus'

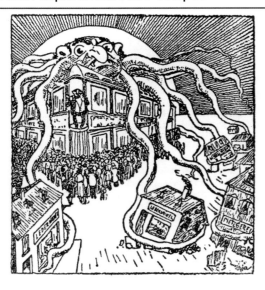

Tasks

1. *What can you learn from Source A about Hitler's attitude to the Jews? (Remember how to answer this type of question? For further guidance see page 20.)*

2. *What is the message of the cartoon in Source B? How does it show one reason why the Nazis persecuted the Jews?*

3. *Look at photos of leading Nazis such as Hitler, Goebbels and Himmler (see pages 14, 24 and 47). Did they fit the image of the ideal Aryan?*

4. *Give two reasons why Hitler decided to persecute the Jews.*

How did the lives of German Jews change in the years 1933–39?

The persecution of the Jews did not begin immediately. Hitler needed to ensure that he had the support of most of the German people for his anti-Semitic policies. This was achieved through propaganda and the use of schools. Young people especially were encouraged to hate Jews, with school lessons and textbooks putting across anti-Semitic views.

Source A Photograph showing Jewish schoolchildren being humiliated in front of their class

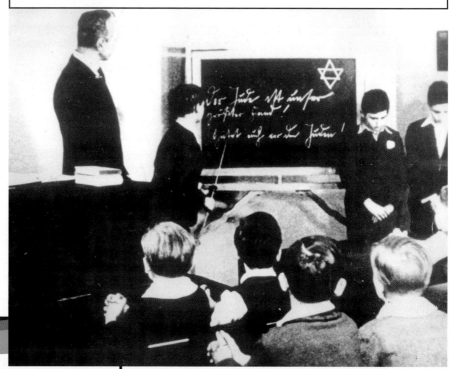

Tasks

1. *How useful are Sources A and B as evidence of how anti-Semitism was taught in schools in Nazi Germany? (Remember how to answer this type of question? For further guidance see pages 51 and 59.)*

2. *Imagine you are a Jewish teenager who kept a diary during the 1930s. Write three to five entries explaining your feelings about Nazi policies. For example, your reactions to the boycott of Jewish shops and the Nuremberg Laws.*

3. *Read page 71. Make a copy of the table below and give examples of measures which removed Jews' political, social or economic rights. One example has been done for you.*

Political	Economic	Social
	Boycott of shops	

Source B Extract from a school textbook

1. The Jewish race is much inferior to the Negro race.
2. All Jews have crooked legs, fat bellies, curly hair and look untrustworthy.
3. The Jews were responsible for the First World War.
4. They are to blame for the treaty of Versailles and hyperinflation.
5. All Jews are Communists.

Measures taken against the Jews

1933

April   The SA organised a boycott of Jewish shops and businesses. They painted 'Jude' (Jew) on windows and tried to persuade the public not to enter.
             Thousands of Jewish civil servants, lawyers and university teachers were sacked.
May   A new law excluded Jews from government jobs.
             Jewish books were burnt.
September   Jews were banned from inheriting land.

1934

Local councils banned Jews from public spaces such as parks, playing fields and swimming pools.

1935

May   Jews were no longer drafted in the army.
June   Restaurants were closed to Jews all over Germany.
September   The Nuremberg Laws were a series of measures aimed against the Jews passed on 15 September. This included the Reich Law on Citizenship, which stated that only those of German blood could be German citizens. Jews lost their citizenship, the right to vote and hold government office. The Law for the Protection of German Blood and Honour forbade marriage or sexual relations between Jews and German citizens.

1936

April   The professional activities of Jews were banned or restricted – this included vets, dentists, accountants, surveyors, teachers and nurses.
July–August There was a deliberate lull in the anti-Jewish campaign as Germany was hosting the Olympics (page 63) and wanted to give the outside world a good impression.

1937

September   For the first time in two years Hitler publicly attacked the Jews.
             More and more Jewish businesses were taken over.

1938

March   Jews had to register their possessions, making it easier to confiscate them.
July   Jews had to carry identity cards. Jewish doctors, dentists and lawyers were forbidden to treat Aryans.
August   Jewish men had to add the name 'Israel' to their first names, Jewish women, the name 'Sarah', to further humiliate them.
October   Jews had the red letter 'J' stamped on their passports.
November   Kristallnacht (see page 72).
             Jewish children were excluded from schools and universities.

Kristallnacht, 9 November 1938

On 8 November 1938 a young Polish Jew, Herschel Grynszpan, walked into the German Embassy in Paris and shot the first official he met. He was protesting against the treatment of his parents in Germany who had been deported to Poland.

Goebbels used this as an opportunity to organise anti-Jewish demonstrations which involved attacks on Jewish property, shops, homes and synagogues. So many windows were smashed in the campaign that the events of 9–10 November became known as *Kristallnacht,* meaning 'Crystal Night' or 'the Night of Broken Glass'. About 100 Jews were killed and 20,000 sent to concentration camps.

The Daily Telegraph
12th November 1938

Mob Law rules
Mob law ruled in Berlin throughout the afternoon and evening as hordes of hooligans took part in an orgy of destruction. I have never seen an anti-Jewish outbreak as sickening as this. I saw fashionably dressed women clapping their hands and screaming with glee while respectable mothers held up their babies to see the 'fun'. No attempt was made by the police to stop the rioters.

Der Stürmer
10th November 1938

Revenge for murder by a Jew
The death of a loyal party member by the Jewish murderer has aroused spontaneous anti-Jewish demonstrations throughout the Reich. In many places Jewish shops have been smashed. The synagogues, from which teachings hostile to the State and People are spread, have been set on fire. Well done to those Germans who have ensured revenge for the murder of an innocent German.

Many Germans were disgusted at *Kristallnacht.* Hitler and Goebbels were anxious that it should not be seen as the work of the Nazis. It was portrayed as a spontaneous act of vengeance by Germans.

The aftermath

Hitler officially blamed the Jews themselves for having provoked the attacks and used this as an excuse to step up the campaign against them. He decreed the following:

Source C A US official describes what he saw in Leipzig

The shattering of shop windows, looting of stores and dwellings of Jews took place in the early hours of 10 November 1938. In one of the Jewish sections an eighteen-year-old boy was hurled from a three-storey window to land with both legs broken on a street littered with broken beds. The main streets of the city were a positive litter of shattered glass. All the synagogues were gutted by flames.

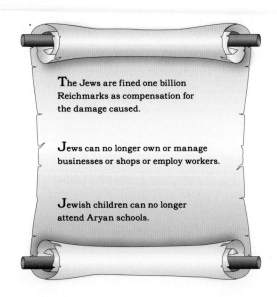

The Jews are fined one billion Reichmarks as compensation for the damage caused.

Jews can no longer own or manage businesses or shops or employ workers.

Jewish children can no longer attend Aryan schools.

The persecution continued in 1939.

- In January the Reich Office for Jewish Emigration was established with Reinhard Heydrich as its director. The SS now had the responsibility for eliminating the Jews from Germany completely. This would be achieved by forced **emigration**. The Nazis wanted other countries to take the Jews as refugees and even discussed a scheme to settle Jews in Madagascar.
- In the following months Jews were required to surrender precious metals and jewellery.
- On 30 April Jews were evicted from their homes and forced into designated Jewish accommodation or **ghettos.**
- In September Jews were forced to hand in their radio sets so they could not listen to foreign news.

Source D A Jewish shop in Berlin, the day after *Kristallnacht*

Tasks

4. *What can you learn from Source C about Kristallnacht? (Remember how to answer this type of question? For further guidance see page 20.)*

5. *In what ways does the German newspaper article in* Der Stürmer *differ from the views expressed by the* Daily Telegraph?

6. *Using a flow diagram show the key changes in the lives of Jews in Germany 1933–39.*

7. *How useful is Source D as evidence of Kristallnacht? (Remember how to answer this type of question? For further guidance see pages 51 and 59.)*

8. *How seriously did the following measures threaten the position of Jews in Nazi Germany? Make a copy of the following table and give a brief explanation for your decisions.*

Event	Rating 1–10 (10 is very serious)	Reason
Boycott of Jewish shops 1933		
Nuremberg Laws		
Kristallnacht 1938		
Deportation 1939		

Which other groups were persecuted?

Ideal Germans were 'socially useful' in that they had a job and contributed to the state. Anyone else was seen as a 'burden on the community'. These included those who could not work, the unhealthy, mentally disabled, tramps and beggars. These people were seen as worthless and expensive to the state and had to be removed.

There were also socially undesirable groups such as alcoholics, homosexuals and juvenile delinquents. They were also seen as dangerous and a bad influence on others. Once again they had to be removed.

Measures taken

As they had with the Jews, the Nazis began with a propaganda campaign to ensure that most German people turned against these undesirables. This was followed by more extreme measures, shown in the boxes below.

Sterilisation Law
Passed in July 1933. It allowed the Nazis to sterilise people with certain illnesses described as 'simple-mindedness' and 'chronic alcoholism'. Between 1934 and 1945 nearly 700,000 men and women were compulsorily sterilised.

Concentration camps
Many 'undesirables' were sent to concentration camps including prostitutes, homosexuals and juvenile delinquents. In 1938 Gypsies, tramps and beggars were added to the list.

Euthanasia campaign
In 1939 the Nazis secretly began to exterminate the mentally ill in a **euthanasia** campaign. Around 6,000 disabled babies, children and teenagers were murdered by starvation or lethal injection.

Source A Commentary from a 1937 Nazi film

Sterilisation is a simple surgical operation. In the last 70 years our people have increased by 50 per cent while in the same period the number of hereditary ill has risen by over 450 per cent. If this was to continue, there would be one hereditary ill person to four healthy people. An endless column of horror would march into the nation.

Source B From a letter to a Frankfurt newspaper from some citizens about the 'Gypsy nuisance'

Right opposite properties Gypsies have settled themselves. They are a heavy burden on the community. The hygienic conditions in this area defy description. We are worried about the spread of contagious diseases. Because of the Gypsies our properties have greatly fallen in value.

The Gypsies

There were about 30,000 **Gypsies** in Germany. The Nazis gave two reasons for removing them:

- They were non-Aryan and threatened racial purity.
- They were homeless and work-shy.

In 1935 the Nazis banned all marriages between Gypsies and Germans. Three years later a Decree for the 'Struggle against the Gypsy Plague' was issued. All Gypsies had to register with the authorities.

Tasks

1. What can you learn from Source B about attitudes to Gypsies in Nazi Germany? (Remember how to answer this type of question? For further guidance see page 20.)

2. What reason is given for sterilisation in Source A?

What opposition was there to Nazi rule?

It is difficult to know how much opposition there was to Nazism in the years 1933 to 1939. The number of people who protested openly against the government is small. Those people must have been incredibly brave.

The government
Von Papen (see page 33) demanded greater freedom in a speech in June 1934 but was purged on the Night of the Long Knives.

The army
A number of army leaders opposed Hitler, especially when he began to break the Treaty of Versailles in the later 1930s by building up the German armed forces and reoccupying the Rhineland. For example, one army leader, General Beck, even planned to arrest Hitler in 1938. His plan was ruined by Hitler's success at the Munich Conference in which he gained an area of Czechoslovakia known as the Sudetenland.

The Churches
(see pages 64–65)
There was opposition from the German Confessional Church and some priests.

OPPOSITION

The youth
(see page 58)
There were teenage rebels such as the Edelweiss Pirates.

Opposition parties
All political parties except the Nazis were banned in July 1933 (see page 42). Nevertheless, the Communists and Social Democrats set up illegal political parties. These were underground organisations which tried to spread resistance among the factory workers.

The workers
Trade unions and strikes were banned. Nevertheless there were an estimated 400 strikes between 1933 and 1935. Many workers kept their links with illegal political parties.

Source A An opposition joke

The ideal German:
As blond as Hitler,
As tall as Goebbels,
As slim as Goering
And as chaste as Röhm.

Tasks

1. *There was little opposition to the Nazis in the 1930s. How important were the following reasons – fear, propaganda, Hitler's achievements? Place each factor somewhere on a copy of this line. Explain your answer.*

←————————————————————→
Decisive   Important   Unimportant

2. *Explain why Source A is a joke.*

Examination practice

Synthesis questions

In question 4 on Paper 2 you are asked to explain an interpretation using:

- six sources
- your own knowledge.

This is known as the synthesis question and is worth the most marks (12). The examiner would expect you to write a minimum of one side of A4. Here is a mark scheme for the synthesis question:

Level	Descriptor	Marks
2	Developed explanation using the sources **or** own knowledge Developed statements using the sources **and** own knowledge	4–7
3	Developed explanation agreeing and/or disagreeing with the interpretation using most of the sources **and** own knowledge	8–10
4	A sustained argument making a balanced judgement using most of the sources **and** own knowledge.	11–12

- If you only use the sources **or** your own knowledge in your answer then the maximum you can be awarded is Level 2. Use both.
- You can achieve a good Level 3 mark (8–10) by agreeing **or** disagreeing as long as you use the sources **and** your own knowledge.
- To reach Level 4 you have to give both sides and use the sources **and** your own knowledge **and** judgement.

Question 1 – synthesis

'*Kristallnacht* was the worst of the anti-Jewish measures during the Nazi persecution in the years 1933 to 1939.'

Study Sources A–F. Use the Sources, and your own knowledge, to explain whether you agree with this view.

Source A Photograph showing the SA enforced boycott of Jewish shops in 1933

Source B From the memoirs of a German mother, written after the Second World War

One day my daughter came home humiliated. 'It was not so nice today.' 'What happened?' I asked. The teacher had sent the Aryan children to one side of the classroom, and the non-Aryans to the other. Then the teacher told the Aryans to study the appearance of the others and to point out the marks of their Jewish race. They stood separated as if by a gulf, children who had played together as friends the day before.

Source C The *Reich* Law on Citizenship, 1935

Only a National of Germany or similar blood, who proves by his behaviour that he is willing and able loyally to serve the German people and Reich *is a citizen of the* Reich. *A Jew may not be a citizen of the* Reich. *He has no vote. He may not hold any public office.*

Source D An illustration from a children's book, warning children not to trust Jews.

Source E The *New York Times*, 11 November 1938

A wave of destruction swept over Germany today. Huge crowds looked on. Generally the crowds were silent and the majority seemed gravely disturbed by the proceedings. Only members of the wrecking squads shouted occasionally 'Perish Jewry!' and 'Kill the Jews!'.

Source F Report of Reinhardt Heydrich, Chief of Security Police, 11 November 1938, on the damage caused by *Kristallnacht*

Shops – 815 destroyed
Synagogues – 276 destroyed
Jews – 20,000 arrested
Looting – 174 looters arrested.
The true figures may be several times greater than those reported.

Planning your answer

Make a copy of the grid below and use it to help you plan your answer. Advice on how to write your answer is given on page 78.

1. First of all, study once again all the sources on pages 76–77.
   - Which sources agree with the interpretation? Why? Give a brief explanation in the grid. An example is given below.
   - Which sources disagree with the interpretation? Why? Give a brief explanation in the grid. An example is given below.

2. Now use your own knowledge of the Nazi measures against the Jews. To help you, look again at page 71.
   - What knowledge can you use to agree with the interpretation? Summarise this in your grid. An example is given in the grid below.
   - What knowledge can you use to disagree with the interpretation? Summarise this in your grid.

3. To help prompt your own knowledge during an examination, underline any dates or facts in the sources which you could expand on in the answer. Expanding on sources will be classed as your own knowledge.

	Agrees with interpretation	Disagrees with interpretation
Source A		
Source B		
Source C		*The Jews were denied German citizenship*
Source D		
Source E		
Source F	*Shows that 815 shops were destroyed and 20,000 Jews were arrested*	
Own knowledge	*Kristallnacht led to even worse measures such as a heavy fine on the Jews*	

Writing your answer

The diagram below shows the steps you should take to write a good synthesis answer.

Use the steps and examples to complete the answer to question 1 on page 76.

STEP 1
Write an introduction that identifies the key issues you need to cover in your answer and your main argument.

Example:
The Nazis introduced a series of measures in the years after 1933 which gradually undermined the position of the Jews in Germany. These culminated in the violence that took place on Kristallnacht. However, other measures, such as the denial of German citizenship, had even more serious consequences.

STEP 2
After your introduction, write a good length paragraph agreeing with the interpretation. Begin each paragraph with a sentence that focuses on the question, followed by your own knowledge. Use at least one of the sources to back up your own knowledge.

Example:
Kristallnacht certainly had a terrible impact on the Jews in Germany. There was considerable damage to Jewish property and a number of Jews were murdered. Source F supports the interpretation, suggesting that 815 shops and 276 synagogues were destroyed and at least 20,000 Jews arrested.

STEP 3
See if you can write another paragraph agreeing with the interpretation, using your own knowledge and possibly a source.

You could explain the measures taken against the Jews after Kristallnacht and also make use of Source E.

Have a go yourself

STEP 4
Write a good length paragraph disagreeing with the interpretation. Begin the paragraph with a sentence that focuses on the question, followed by your own knowledge. Use at least one of the sources to back up your own knowledge.

Example:
However, other measures had worse effects on the Jews. For example, from 1933 Goebbels organised a systematic programme of anti-Jewish propaganda which aimed to turn people against the Jews. Jews were portrayed as evil and blamed for all of Germany's recent problems, including the Depression. One example of such propaganda is Source D which suggests that the Jews are evil and kidnap children.

STEP 5
See if you can write another paragraph disagreeing with the interpretation, using your own knowledge and possibly a source.

You could explain the boycott of Jewish shops and use Source A.

Have a go yourself

STEP 6
Write a conclusion giving your final judgement on the interpretation. Do you mainly agree or disagree? Explain your judgement.

Example:
For the most part I disagree with the interpretation. I believe that there was no one measure that was worse than the others but the accumulation of a variety of Nazi measures, such as propaganda, anti-Jewish laws and events such as Kristallnacht, eventually made the Jews' lives unbearable.

6 The social impact of Nazism

> **Source A** Nazi poster of 1937 showing the central role of women. It says 'The Nazi Party protects the national community'

> **Source B** Social Democrat Party poster. It says 'Women, this is what your life will be like in the Third Reich'

Tasks

1. *What does Source A suggest the role of women was in Nazi Germany?*

2. *Does Source B have the same views? Explain your answer.*

The Nazis tried to radically change the role of women in society. They opposed the progress women had made and wanted them to revert to a traditional domestic role. To what extent did they achieve this? Hitler, through a variety of methods, kept his promise to achieve full employment. However, were workers better off under the Nazis?

This chapter answers the following questions:

- What was the Nazi view of the role of women?
- How did the role of women change under the Nazis?
- How successful were these policies?

- What policies were introduced to reduce unemployment?
- Were German people better or worse off under the Nazis?

Source skills

You will be given the opportunity to practise all four source questions from Paper 2.

What was the Nazi view of the role of women?

Changes during the Weimar Republic

Women had made significant progress in their position in German society during the 1920s.

Political	Economic	Social
Women over 20 were given the vote and took an increasing interest in politics. By 1933 one tenth of the members of the *Reichstag* were female.	Many took up careers in the professions, especially the civil service, law, medicine and teaching. Those who worked in the civil service earned the same as men. By 1933 there were 100,000 women teachers and 3,000 doctors.	Socially, they went out unescorted, drank and smoked in public, were slim and fashion conscious, often wearing relatively short skirts, had their hair cut short and wore make up.

Nazi ideals

The Nazis had a very traditional view of the role of women, very different from women's position in society in the 1920s.

German women in a bar, 1930

The Nazi ideal woman
- Did not wear make up
- Was blonde, heavy hipped and athletic
- Wore flat shoes and a full skirt
- Did not smoke
- Did not go out to work
- Did all the household duties especially cooking and bringing up the children
- Took no interest in politics

Source A Goebbels describes the role of women in 1929

The mission of women is to be beautiful and to bring children into the world. The female bird pretties herself for her mate and hatches eggs for him. In exchange, the male takes care of gathering the food and stands guard and wards off the enemy.

Source B A German rhyme addressed to women

Take hold of the kettle, broom and pan,
Then you'll surely get a man!
Shop and office leave alone,
Your true life work lies at home.

Tasks

1. What can you learn from Source A about the Nazi view of the role of women? (Remember how to answer this type of question? For further guidance see page 20.)

2. Does Source B support Source A about the Nazi view of the role of women? Explain your answer. (Remember how to answer this type of question? For further guidance see pages 36–37.)

3. Draw sketches of two women.

- Label the first sketch with the features of a 'modern woman' during the 1920s.
- Label the second with the Nazi view of women.

How did the role of women change under the Nazis?

The Nazis brought in a series of measures to change the role of women.

Marriage and family

The Nazis were very worried by the decline in the birth rate. In 1900 there had been over 2 million live births per year but this had dropped to under 1 million in 1933.

- A massive propaganda campaign was launched to promote motherhood and large families.
- In 1933 the Law for the Encouragement of Marriage was introduced. This aimed to increase Germany's falling birth-rate by giving loans to help young couples to marry provided the wife left her job. Couples were allowed to keep one quarter of the loan for each child born up to four.
- On Hitler's mother's birthday (12 August) medals were awarded to women with large families.
- In 1938 they changed the divorce law – a divorce was possible if a husband or wife could not have children.
- The Nazis also set up the *Lebensborn* (Life Springs) programme whereby specially chosen unmarried women could 'donate a baby to the *Führer*' by becoming pregnant by 'racially pure' SS men.
- A new national organisation, the German Women's Enterprise, organised classes and radio talks on household topics and the skills of motherhood.

Jobs

Instead of going to work, women were asked to stick to the 'three Ks' – *Kinder, Küche, Kirche* – 'children, kitchen, church'. The Nazis had another incentive to get women to give up work. They had been elected partly because they promised more jobs. Every job left by a woman, returning to the home, was available for a man.

Women doctors, civil servants and teachers were forced to leave their jobs. Schoolgirls were trained for work at home (page 56). They were discouraged from going on to higher education.

However, from 1937, the Nazis had to reverse these policies. Germany was rearming. Men were joining the army. Now they needed more women to go out to work. They abolished the marriage loans and introduced a compulsory 'duty year' for all women entering employment. This usually meant helping on a farm or in a family home in return for bed and board but no pay. This change of policy was not very successful. By 1939 there were fewer women working than there had been under the Weimar Republic.

Appearance

Women were encouraged to keep healthy and wear their hair in a bun or plaits. They were discouraged from wearing trousers, high heels and make-up, from dyeing or styling their hair, and from slimming, as this was seen as bad for childbearing.

Source A German cartoon from the 1930s. The caption reads 'Introducing Frau Mueller who up to now has brought 12 children into the world'

"Und hier stelle ich Euch Frau Müller vor, die bis jetzt 12 Kinder zur Welt gebracht hat!"

Source B A Nazi pamphlet sent to young German women

1. Remember that you are a German.

2. If you are genetically healthy, you should get married.

3. Keep your body pure.

4. Keep your mind and spirit pure.

5. Marry only for love.

6. As a German choose only a husband of similar or related blood.

7. In choosing a husband, ask about his ancestors.

8. Health is essential for physical beauty.

9. Don't look for a playmate but for a companion in marriage.

10. You should want to have as many children as possible.

Source C Marianne Gartner was a member of the League of German Maidens and remembers one of its meetings in 1936

At one meeting the team leader raised her voice. 'There is no greater honour for a German woman than to bear children for the Führer and for the Fatherland! The Führer has ruled that no family will be complete without at least four children. A German woman does not use make-up! A German woman does not smoke! She has a duty to keep herself fit and healthy! Any questions?' 'Why isn't the Führer married and a father himself?' I asked.

Tasks

1. *What message is the cartoonist trying to put across in Source A?*

2. *How useful is Source B as evidence of the role of women in Nazi Germany?*
(Remember how to answer this type of question? For further guidance see pages 51 and 59.)

3. *What can you learn from Source C about the role of women in Nazi Germany? (Remember how to answer this type of question? For further guidance see page 20.)*

Nazi Germany 1930–1939

How successful were these policies?

Source A Extract from a letter from several women to a Leipzig newspaper in 1934

Today man is educated not for, but against, marriage. We see our daughters growing up in stupid aimlessness living only in a vague hope of getting a man and having children. A son, even the youngest, laughs in his mother's face. He regards her as his servant and women in general are merely willing tools of his aims.

Source B From Toni Christen, an American journalist writing in 1939

I talked to Mrs Schmidt, a woman of about 50, as she came out of the shop. 'You see, older women are no good in Germany,' she said. 'We are no longer capable of bearing children. We have no value to the state. They don't care for us mothers or grandmothers any more. We are worn out, discarded.'

Source C From Judith Grunfeld, an American journalist, 1937

How many women workers did the Führer send home? According to the statistics of the German Department of Labour, there were in June 1936, 5,470,000 employed women, or 1,200,000 more than in January 1933. The Nazi campaign has not been successful in reducing the numbers of women employed. It has simply squeezed them out of better paid positions into the sweated trades. This type of labour with its miserable wages and long hours is extremely dangerous to the health of women and degrades the family.

Source D Employment of women in millions

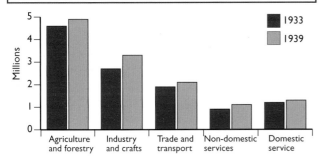

Source E The views of Wilhelmine Haferkamp who was 22 in 1933. She lived in the industrial city of Oberhausen

When one had ten children, well not ten but a pile of them, one had to join the Nazi Party. 1933 it was and I already had three children and the fourth on the way. When 'child-rich' people were in the Party the children had a great chance to advance. I got 30 marks per child from the Hitler government and 20 marks per child from the city. That was a lot of money. I sometimes got more 'child money' than my husband earned.

Tasks

1. Make a copy of the following table. Sort Sources A–E into successes and failures for Nazi policies in the areas of marriage/family and jobs. Complete the grid with an explanation of your choices. One has been done for you.

	Success	**Failure**
Marriage and family		*Source B as the Nazis did not value older women*
Jobs		

2. You are a British journalist who has visited Nazi Germany in 1938 to investigate the role of women. Use the work you have done on task 1 to write an article explaining the successes and failures of Nazi policies. You will need a catchy headline. You could include imaginary interviews.

3. 'The Nazi policies were successful in changing the position of women in society.' Using Sources A–E and your own knowledge explain whether you agree with this view. (Remember how to answer this type of question? For further guidance see page 76.)

What policies were introduced to reduce unemployment?

Hitler introduced a series of measures to reduce unemployment.

The Labour Service Corps

Source A Young men in the Labour Service carrying out military drill in 1933

Source C An official photograph showing workers gathering to begin work on the first autobahn, September 1933

This was a scheme to provide young men with manual labour jobs. From 1935 it was compulsory for all men aged 18–25 to serve in the corps for six months. Workers lived in camps, wore uniforms, received very low pay and carried out military drill as well as work.

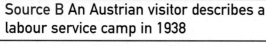

Source B An Austrian visitor describes a labour service camp in 1938

The camps are organised on thoroughly military lines. The youths wear uniforms like soldiers. The only difference is that they carry spades instead of rifles and work in the fields.

Job creation schemes

Hitler at first spent millions on job creation schemes, rising from 18.4 billion marks in 1933 to 37.1 billion five years later. The Nazis subsidised private firms, especially in the construction industry. They also introduced a massive road-building programme to provide Germany with 7,000km of autobahns (motorways).

Invisible unemployment

The Nazis used some dubious methods to keep down the unemployment figures. The official figures did not include the following:

- Jews dismissed from their jobs
- unmarried men under 25 who were pushed into National Labour schemes
- women dismissed from their jobs or who gave up work to get married
- opponents of the Nazi regime held in concentration camps.

The figures also included part-time workers as fully employed.

Rearmament

Hitler was determined to build up the armed forces in readiness for future war. This, in turn, greatly reduced unemployment.

THE ROAD TO FULL EMPLOYMENT

- The re-introduction of **conscription** in 1935 took thousands of young men into military service. The army grew from 100,000 in 1933 to 1,400,000 by 1939.
- Heavy industry expanded to meet the needs of rearmament. Coal and chemicals doubled in the years 1933 to 1939; oil, iron and steel trebled.
- Billions were spent producing tanks, aircraft and ships. In 1933, 3.5 billion marks were spent on rearmament. This had increased to 26 billion marks by 1939.

Tasks

1. *Does Source B support the evidence of Source A about National Labour Service? Explain your answer. (Remember how to answer this type of question? For further guidance see page 36.)*

2. *Study Source C. Why do you think this photograph was taken?*

3. *What does Source D suggest about the German army? (Remember how to answer this type of question? For further guidance see page 20.)*

Source D A photograph of German armed forces

Were German people better or worse off under the Nazis?

Better off

Strength through Joy (*Kraft durch Freude* – KdF)

This was an organisation set up by the German Labour Front to replace trade unions. The KdF tried to improve the leisure time of German workers by sponsoring a wide range of leisure and cultural trips. These included concerts, theatre visits, museum tours, sporting events, weekend trips, holidays and cruises. All were provided at a low cost giving ordinary workers access to activities normally reserved for the better off.

Source A Official figures for numbers taking part in KdF activities in 1938

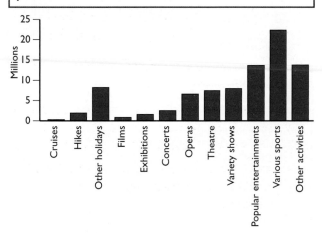

Beauty of Work

This was a department of the KdF that tried to improve working conditions. It organised the building of canteens, swimming pools and sports facilities. It also installed better lighting in the workplace.

Source B German workers on a KdF cruise in 1935

Volkswagen scheme

In 1938 the Labour Front organised the Volkswagen (people's car) scheme, giving workers an opportunity to subscribe 5 marks a week to a fund eventually allowing them to acquire a car.

Wages

Average weekly wages rose from 86 marks in 1932 to 109 marks in 1938.

Food consumption

Source C Consumption per head of selected foods

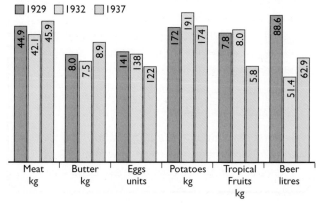

Tasks

1. What can you learn from Source A about the KdF? (Remember how to answer this type of question? For further guidance see page 20.)

2. Does Source B support Source A about the popularity of Strength through Joy? Explain your answer. (Remember how to answer this type of question? For further guidance see page 36.)

3. Does Source C suggest that people were better off under the Nazis? Explain your answer.

Worse off

Lack of freedom

German workers lost their rights under the Nazis. In 1933 trade unions were banned (see page 75). This meant workers could no longer negotiate for better pay or reduced hours of work and strikes were banned. Those who opposed the Nazis were rounded up and sent to concentration camps for 're-education'.

Strength through Joy

Very few workers could actually afford the more expensive activities such as cruises to Madeira and Scandinavia. Beauty of Work caused much resentment as workers had to carry out improvements in their spare time and without pay.

Volkswagen swindle

This idea to encourage people to save to buy a Volkswagen was a con-trick. People were encouraged to save 5 marks per week to buy their own car. By the time war broke out in 1939 not a single customer had taken delivery of a car. None of the money was refunded.

Cost of living

The cost of living increased during the 1930s. All basic groceries, except fish, cost more in 1939 than they had in 1933. Food items were in short supply partly because it was government policy to reduce agricultural production. This was to keep up the prices for the benefit of the farmers.

Hours of work

The average working hours in industry increased from 42.9 per week in 1933 to 47 in 1939.

> **Source D** A French cartoon of 1934. The caption reads 'What! Bread? Don't you know the Nazi revolution is over?'

Tasks

4. What message is the cartoonist trying to get across in Source D?

5. Work in pairs. Imagine you interview a German worker in 1938. You are trying to find out how his lifestyle has changed under the Nazis.

- *Think of three questions you would ask him.*
- *Write down possible answers to the questions.*

6. Make a copy of this pair of scales and write in evidence of German workers being better or worse off. Overall, what does your pair of scales reveal?

BETTER OFF   WORSE OFF

Examination practice

Source skills

Here is your opportunity to practise all four source questions.

Source A From the memoirs of a German who experienced Labour Service, 1936

We started physical exercise at a ridiculously early time. Before and after work we got military drill and instruction. We worked outdoors in all kinds of weather for the sum of only 51 pfennigs an hour. Then they took off deductions and voluntary contributions, including 15 pfennigs for a straw mattress and draughty barracks and 35 pfennigs for what they ladle out of a cauldron and call dinner – slop – you wouldn't touch it, I guarantee it.

Source C Report from the Social Democratic Party on Labour Service, 1938

The young people are deadened by physical exertion. They have to get up very early and have very little time to themselves. The whole aim of the service seems to be to pass on Nazi ideas and prepare them for military service. The pay is pitiful. Barely enough to buy a beer.

Source D Extract from the Strength through Joy magazine, 1936

KdF is now running weekly theatre trips to Munich from the countryside. Special theatre trains are coming to Munich on weekdays from as far away as 120km. So a lot of our comrades who used to be in the Outdoor Club, for example, are availing themselves of the opportunity of going on trips with KdF. There is simply no other choice. Walking trips have also become very popular.

Source B The daily programme in a Labour Front camp in 1938

```
04.45 . . . . . . Get up.
04.50 . . . . . Gymnastics.
05.15 . . . . . . Wash and make beds.
05.30 . . . . . Coffee break.
05.50 . . . . . . Parade.
6.00 . . . . . . March to building site.
Work till 14.30 with 30 minutes break for breakfast.
15.00 . . . . . . Lunch.
15.30–18.00 . Drill.
18.10–1845 . . . Instruction.
18.45–19.15 . . Cleaning and mending.
19.15 . . . . . . Parade.
19.30 . . . . . . Announcements.
19.45 . . . . . . Supper.
20.00–21.30 . Sing-song or other leisure activities.
22.00 . . . . . Lights out.
```

Source E A Strength through Joy poster of 1938 encouraging German workers to go on cruises

Die Deutsche Arbeitsfront

Urlauberfahrten
zur See

N.S.-Gemeinschaft »Kraft durch Freude«

Tasks

1. *Study Source A.*
What can you learn from Source A about Labour Service under the Nazis? (4 marks)
(Remember how to answer this type of question? For further guidance see page 20.)

2. Study Sources A, B and C.
Does Source C support the evidence of Sources A and B about Labour Service under the Nazis? Explain your answer. (6 marks)
(Remember how to answer this type of question? For further guidance see page 36.)

3. *Study Sources D and E.*
How useful are these two sources as evidence about the Strength through Joy movement?
(8 marks)
(Remember how to answer this type of question? For further guidance see pages 51 and 59.)

4. *Study all the Sources.*
'The Nazis greatly improved the lifestyle of German workers.'
Use the sources and your own knowledge to explain whether you agree with this view.
(12 marks)
(Remember how to answer this type of question? For further guidance see page 76.)

(Total 30 marks)

Source F From a modern history of Germany, published in 1997

German workers were not necessarily better off than they had been under the Weimar Republic. It is true that unemployment reached a lower level than in Britain, but this was due to invisible unemployment as well as conscription and compulsory Labour Service. Workers had little freedom and most had to work longer hours.

Revision activities

Chapter 1

1. Explain, in no more than a sentence, what you know about the following:

    a. *Dolchstoss*
    b. Spartacists
    c. *Freikorps*
    d. Article 231: The War Guilt Clause
    e. hyperinflation
    f. how to begin the answer of an inference question.

2. Place the following events in chronological order:

    ☐ Hitler jailed
    ☐ Treaty of Versailles signed
    ☐ Hitler became leader of the NSDAP
    ☐ Reparations figure announced
    ☐ Armistice signed
    ☐ Beer Hall *Putsch*

3. Match the words to the definition.

    Words: **swastika, November Criminals, *Volksgemeinschaft*, *Dolchstoss***

    Definitions:
    **stab in the back
    hooked cross
    People's Community
    those who signed the armistice**

4. Summarise in no more than ten words the importance of the following for Hitler.

The Munich *Putsch*	
Imprisonment	
The Bamberg Conference	

5. Summarise in no more than ten words the following problems faced by the Weimar government.

Proportional representation	
Hyperinflation	
Treaty of Versailles	
Political unrest	

Chapter 2

1. The following account of Hitler's rise to power is by a student who has not revised thoroughly. Re-write the account, correcting any errors.

    The Depression hit Germany in 1928. So Germany borrowed money from the USA because there was hyperinflation. Chancellor Hindenburg got the Reichstag to pass decrees to solve the problems. Hitler then took over in 1932 because he had won more than 50 per cent of the seats.

2. Are the following statements about the Nazis' election methods during the years 1930–32 true or false?

	True	False
They advertised on television		
They used huge numbers of posters across Germany		
They used violence only in order to defend themselves		
They used modern technology		
Hitler kept his message simple		

3. Make a copy of the following grid and give at least three reasons in each column to show how each helped Hitler to come to power.

Treaty of Versailles	The Great Depression	Political intrigue

4. For the following two statements, write a paragraph on each explaining why you agree with it.

Hitler's own personal attraction and speaking ability were the main reasons why he won the support of the people.

Fear of Communism in Germany was the main reason Hitler won the support of many people.

Chapter 3

1.

a. 'The *Reichstag* Fire was a Communist plot.' Write two or three sentences agreeing with this statement.
b. 'The *Reichstag* Fire was organised by the Nazis.' Write two or three sentences agreeing with this statement.

2. Make a copy of the following grid and in ten words or less summarise why each was important for the Nazis.

The SA	
Enabling Law	
Support of the army	
Concentration camps	

3. Decide whether the following statements are causes or effects of the Night of the Long Knives.

	Cause	Effect
Hitler needed the support of the army		
Röhm was too powerful		
The SS and Gestapo became stronger		
Terror grew		
The SA wanted a social revolution		
Hitler had fewer opponents		
Goering wanted to lead all the armed forces		

4. Who or what were the following?

Marinus van der Lubbe
The Law against the Formation of Political Parties
Dachau, 1933
The meaning of the word *Führer*

5. Place the following events in chronological order – for accuracy, give the month and the year in your answer.

☐ Night of the Long Knives
☐ Hitler took the title of *Führer*
☐ Enabling Law
☐ *Reichstag* Fire
☐ Death of President Hindenburg

Chapter 4

1. Make a copy of the following grid and in no more than ten words summarise Nazi changes.

Art	
Architecture	
Music	
Theatre	
Films	

2. The following account of Nazi propaganda is by a student who has not revised thoroughly. Re-write the account, correcting any errors.

In 1933 Hermann Goering was made Minister of Propaganda. He organised a massive annual rally at a place called Stuttgart. In May 1933 students and members of the SA organised a mass book burning. They mainly burnt copies of Mein Kampf. Expensive radios were produced so that only a few Germans could hear Nazi broadcasts.

1. Summarise in no more than ten words the following examples of the treatment of the Jews.

Kristallnacht	
The Nuremberg Laws	
Boycott of Jewish shops	
Local councils	
Forenames	

3. Are the following statements about Hitler's policies towards the young true or false?

	True	False
Boys and girls were taught in separate schools		
Children started the Hitler Youth at the age of eight		
Very little PE was taught in schools		
At the age of fourteen girls joined the League of German Maidens		
Teachers had to join the Nazi Teachers' League		

2. Place the following events in chronological order:
   - ☐ *Kristallnacht*
   - ☐ Boycott of Jewish shops
   - ☐ The Nuremberg Laws
   - ☐ Local councils banning Jews in public places

3. Match the words to the definition.

   Words: **euthanasia, anti-Semitism, Aryan, subhuman**

   Definitions:
   Hatred of or policies against the Jews
   Tall, blond and blue-eyed
   According to the Nazis, members of the underclass such as Jews and Slavs
   Act of killing someone to relieve suffering

4. The following sentences should be paired together.

a. A great many Protestants refused to support the Nazis.
b. Hitler soon broke his agreement with the Pope.
c. Some Protestants, led by Pastor Ludwig Müller, supported the Nazis.

i. They set up the 'German Christians'.
ii. They were led by Pastor Niemöller and set up the German Confessional Church.
iii. He began to persecute the Catholic Church by closing their schools and youth movements.

4. How did the Nazis justify their persecution of:
   - Gypsies
   - the disabled and mentally ill
   - tramps and the unemployed?

5. 'There was no opposition to the Third Reich, 1933–36.' Write a paragraph disagreeing with this statement and including examples of opposition.

5. Explain, in no more than a sentence, what you know about the following:

   The German Young People   The Berlin Olympics
   Hitler Youth activities   The nature of a source
   The Edelweiss Pirates   The origin of a source

6. There is always more than one interpretation of an event. Here are some interpretations of various events. Add your own interpretation of each to the list.

Interpretation	Your own
The main reason Hitler persecuted the Jews was because of his life in Vienna.	
Goebbels was the main reason that *Kristallnacht* took place.	
The worst effect of *Kristallnacht* was damage to Jewish property.	
Gypsies suffered more than any other minority groups under the Nazis.	

Chapter 6

1. Make a copy of the following table and, using key words, summarise the main differences between the role of women before and after 1933.

	Before 1933	After 1933
Marriage and children		
Work		
Appearance		

2. The Nazis claimed that women were not second-class citizens but were given a very important role in Nazi Germany. Write down three examples of this important role.

3. Choose one of the following interpretations of women in Nazi Germany and write a paragraph justifying the statement.

- There was considerable change in the position of women under the Nazis.
- There was some change in the position of women under the Nazis.
- There was little change in the position of women under the Nazis.

4. What explanation can you give for the following contradictory statements?

- The Nazis wanted to reduce the number of women working yet there were more employed in 1939 than in 1933.
- Workers' wages were higher in 1939 than in 1933 yet they were worse off money wise.
- Many Jews and women lost their jobs after 1933 yet unemployment figures went down.

5. What were the following?

a. Beauty of Work
b. Strength through Joy
c. The Labour Front
d. Labour Service
e. The Volkswagen scheme

6. Were German workers better off under the Nazis? Make a copy of the Venn diagram below and fill it in.

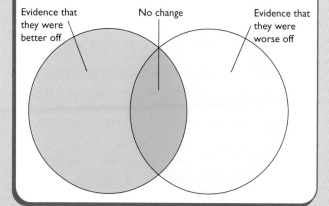

Evidence that they were better off | No change | Evidence that they were worse off

Glossary

anti-Semitism Hatred and persecution of the Jews

armistice The ending of hostilities in a war

Aryan Nazi term for a non-Jewish German, someone of supposedly 'pure' German stock

Bolshevism Named from the Bolsheviks, members of the Russian Social Democrat Party, who followed Lenin

capitalism An economic system in which the production and distribution of goods depend on private investment

censorship Controlling what is produced and suppressing anything considered to be against the state

Centre Party Catholic Party occupying the middle ground in political views

civil rights Basic rights of citizens such as the right to vote, equal treatment under the law, etc.

coalition government A government of two or more political parties

Communist Party (KPD) The German Communist Party, following the ideas of Karl Marx

Communists Those followers of the Communist ideas of Karl Marx believing e.g. that the state should own the means of production and distribution

concentration camp Prison for political prisoners and enemies of the state, who are placed there without trial

concordat Agreement

conscription Compulsory military service for a certain period of time

constitution The basic principles according to which a country is governed

DAP (*Deutsche Arbeiter Partei*) The German Workers' Party

Dawes Plan Introduced in 1924 to reduce Germany's annual reparation payments

decree An order or legal statement made by the President without reference to the *Reichstag*

DNVP (*Deutschnationale Volkspartei*) The German National People's Party, the nationalist right-wing party supported by business people and landowners

Dolchstoss Stab in the back

emigration Moving to another country

Enabling Bill The Bill that gave Hitler the power to rule for four years without consulting the *Reichstag*

euthanasia The bringing about of death to relieve suffering. The Nazis interpreted this as killing anyone who was seen as substandard and of no further use to the state

federal structure System in which power is divided between a central government (*Reichstag*) and regional governments (*Länder*)

Freikorps Private armies set up by senior German army officers at the end of the First World War. They mainly comprised ex-soldiers

Gestapo (*Geheime Staatspolizei*) Secret State Police

ghetto A densely populated area of a city inhabited by a particular ethnic group, such as Jews

Gleichschaltung Bringing people into the identical way of thinking and behaving. Usually translated as co-ordination

Great Depression Slump in the economy which led to high unemployment

Gypsy A race of people scattered throughout Europe who believe in moving round rather than living in one place

Heil Hitler Form of salute to Hitler

Hitler Youth Organisation set up for the young in Germany to convert them to Nazi ideas

hyperinflation Extremely high inflation, where the value of money plummets and it becomes almost worthless

indoctrination Converting people to your ideas using education and propaganda

informant Person who gives information to the authorities about the activities of other people

Länder Regional states of Germany

League of Nations The international body established after the Great War in order to maintain peace

Lebensraum Living space; aim of German expansion in the east

left-wing Of politicians/parties which favour socialism

manifesto A public declaration of a political party's policies

Marxist Follower of the ideas of Karl Marx, closely allied to Communism

National Socialist Member of the NSDAP

nationalise To change from private ownership to state ownership

Nationalist Party Shortened form of the German National People's Party (DNVP)

Nazi Labour Front Organisation set up by Nazis to control German workers

Nazi Teachers' League Organisation set up to control teachers and what they taught

Nazi-Nationalist government Coalition of NSDAP and DNVP after January 1933

plebiscite Direct vote of the electorate on an important public issue

proportional representation The number of votes won in an election determined the number of seats in the *Reichstag*

purge Removal of opponents

Putsch Attempted takeover of the government

Reich In German, this has many meanings – state, kingdom, empire. When used by the Nazis it tended to mean empire or Germany

Reichstag German state parliament

reparations War damages to be paid by Germany

SA (*Sturmabteilung*) The stormtroopers of the Nazi Party

scapegoat A person or group made to take the blame for others

SD (*Sicherheitsdienst*) Security Service

Slav Member of any of the peoples of Eastern Europe

Social Democrats (SPD) Main left-wing party, supported mainly by the working class

Socialists Those who believe in state ownership

Spartacist Extreme left-wing members of the SPD

SS (*Schutzstaffel*) Originally, Hitler's private bodyguard; eventually grew to have very wide-ranging powers

Third Reich Nazi name for Germany. Meant Third Empire

trade unions Organisations set up to protect and improve the rights of workers

treason A crime committed against the state

Volksgemeinschaft The people's community. This was the Nazi idea of a community based upon the German race

Index

architecture 62
army 43
   rearmament 85
art 62
Aryan race 62, 63, 68

Bielenberg, Christabel 21
books 55
Brüning, Chancellor 23

Catholic Church 53, 64
censorship 6
Centre Party 32, 64
cinema 54
Clemenceau, G. 11
Communists 8, 12, 64
   and the Enabling Bill 42
   and the *Reichstag* Fire 41
   and the SA 17, 29
concentration camps 42, 74

DAP (German Workers' Party) 15
Dawes Plan 22
Dolchstoss theory 8, 15, 33
Drexler, Anton 15, 16

Ebert, Friedrich 8, 9, 10, 42
Edelweiss Pirates 4, 58, 75
education 56, 61
employment
   Nazi policies on 84–5
   and women 81
Enabling Bill 42
euthanasia campaign 74

family life 81–3
food prices 87
Freikorps 8, 12

German Confessional Church 75
German Socialist Party 8
Gestapo 47, 48
girls and the Nazi state 57, 61, 82
Gleichschaltung 42, 47–50
Goebbels, Josef 19, 24, 26, 28, 41, 52, 54–5, 80
Goering, Hermann 40, 41, 44, 46, 48
Great Depression 22–3, 25
Great War (1914–18) 7, 8, 15, 18
Gypsies 74

Heydrich, Reinhard 73
Himmler, Heinrich 18, 47, 48

Hindenburg, Paul von 23, 26, 32, 33, 34, 40, 43
Hitler, Adolf
   anti-semitism 19, 67, 68, 69
   and the army 43
   becomes Chancellor 4, 21, 32–5
   biography 14
   involvement in the Nazi Party 14–17
   Munich Beer Hall *Putsch* 12, 18
   and the Presidential election (1932) 26
   in prison 18, 19
   speeches 30–1
Hitler Youth 54, 57, 58, 62
Hugenberg, Alfred 28
hyperinflation 12–13, 20

Jews
   Hitler's anti-semitism 19, 67, 68, 69
   and Nazi Party policy 19, 21, 27
   persecution of 70–3, 76, 77
judges 49–50

KdF (Strength through Joy) 86, 87, 88, 89
Kristallnacht (Night of Broken Glass) 4, 72–3, 77

Labour Service Corps 84, 88
Länder parliaments 42
legal system 49–50
Ludendorff, General 18

marriage and family life 81–3
Mein Kampf (Hitler) 15, 19, 25, 61
Müller, Ludwig 64–5
Munich Beer Hall *Putsch* 12, 18
music 62

Nazi Labour Front 42
Nazi Party
   25 Point Programme 16, 19, 30, 45
   changes (1924–9) 19
   electoral success 25, 29, 32–3, 36
   financial support for 28
   Hitler as leader 16–17, 19
   origins 15
   propaganda 24
   rise to power (1929–33) 21
newspapers 54, 55
Night of the Long Knives 4, 43, 44–6, 48
NOP (nature, origin, purpose) of sources 6, 39, 51, 59–60

November Criminals 8, 14, 18, 25
Nuremberg rallies 30, 54, 66

Olympics (1936) 62–3
opposition to Nazi rule 75
Owens, Jesse 4, 63

Papen, Franz von 32, 33, 34, 40, 75
parliamentary democracy, end of 40–1
Pius XI, Pope 64
police state 47–8
propaganda 24, 53–5, 67
Protestant Church 53, 64–5

racial state theory 68
radios 54
Reichstag (German Parliament) 23
   elections (1932) 26, 28, 29, 32–3
   Fire (1933) 4, 40, 41
Röhm, Ernst 44, 45
Rosenberg, Alfred 19

SA (Sturmabteilung) 17, 28, 29, 44–6, 71
Scheidemann, Philipp 8
Schleicher, Kurt von 34
SD (Security Service) 47, 48
Spartacist uprising (1919) 8
SPD (Social Democratic Party) 23
Speer, Albert 31, 38
sport 62–3
SS (Schutzstaffel) 44, 48
sterilisation law 74
Strasser, Gregor 19
Stresemann, Gustav 13, 22
swastika, the 17, 52

trade unions 75, 87

unemployment 22–3, 84–5, 89

Versailles, Treaty of 7, 10–11, 15, 19, 25, 56
Volkswagen scheme 86, 87

Weimar Republic 7, 10, 12–13, 18, 25
   constitution 9
   economic crisis 23
   and women 80
women 79–83

young people and the Nazi state 53, 56–8